Create Your Own
JAPANESE GARDEN

Create Your Own
JAPANESE
GARDEN

A Practical Guide

Motomi Oguchi
with Joseph Cali

TRANSLATED BY Kay Yokota

KODANSHA INTERNATIONAL
Tokyo • New York • London.

CONTENTS

Distributed in the United States by Kodansha America Inc., and in the United Kingdom and continental Europe by Kodansha Europe Ltd.

Published by Kodansha International Ltd., 17–14 Otowa 1-chome, Bunkyo-ku, Tokyo 112–8652, and Kodansha America, Inc.

Text copyright © 2007 by Motomi Oguchi and Joseph Cali. All photographs except those by Joseph Cali copyright © 2007 by Motomi Oguchi. All rights reserved. Printed in Japan.
ISBN 978–4–7700–2804–4

First edition, 2007
15 14 13 12 11 10 09 08 07   10 9 8 7 6 5 4 3 2 1

Library of Congress Cataloging-in-Publication Data available

www.kodansha-intl.com

The Intimate Relationship of House and Garden

This is a practical guide to applying typical Japanese garden styles to your home or business. The images and techniques in this book present a variety of ways to integrate home and garden in a natural and comfortable way. Japanese homes are world famous for their small size. Yet, no matter how small, gardens bring their owners into intimate contact with nature, even in the midst of urban sprawl.

The history of the Japanese garden is linked to three main factors: the influences of property size, the relationship to architecture, and the physical conditions of the Kyoto region in which much of Japanese garden design and technique developed. Of these three factors, the first two are integrally linked in that changes in architecture have often come in response to shrinking property sizes.

Of the three main representative architectural styles with strong bearing on the garden—*shinden*, *shoin*, and *sukiya*—the *shinden* style is the oldest and most palatial of the three. This style was prevalent from the Ancient through the Classical eras. The *shinden* style consisted of a large central building (*shinden*) connected to smaller outlying buildings (*tainoya*) through open corridors (*sukiro*)—in a more or less symmetrical layout. Inside the *shinden* there was a large, central room called a *moya*, surrounded by a wide corridor-like space called a *hisashi*. The walls to the south side, facing the garden, were filled with *shitomido* and *tsumado* doors that were hinged on top and opened upward. Surrounding the exterior was an *ochi-en* open corridor, covered by a roof and usually containing a balustrade. The combination produced a panoramic view of the garden and a continuous flow of space from exterior to interior. This group of buildings normally sat on the northern half of a 1- to 2-*cho* site (approx. 3.5 to 7 acres/14,400 to 28,800 sqm).

The ideal garden of this time is detailed in the oldest existing book on garden design, the eleventh century *Sakuteiki*. This *tsukiyama* (artificial hill) style garden, was made up of a large pond for boating, islands, artificial hills and streams, waterfalls, plantings, and stone settings. The size of this garden was probably half of the 1-*cho* site (about 1.7 acres/7,200 sqm) and up to half of that was set aside for a flat, sand-covered area between the building and the pond.

But even in the Classical era, the size of the largest estates was already being reduced, and larger property sizes of one-quarter *cho* (about 4,305 square yards/3,600 sqm) or less, were common. Both architecture and the garden changed to adjust to these conditions. The symmetrical layout becomes asymmetric (the so-called "Flight of Geese" pattern), and garden features, such as ponds and islands, are abbreviated and abstracted.

A garden and *sukiya* style home built in the mid 1900s, now restored and serving as a *sento* (bathhouse).

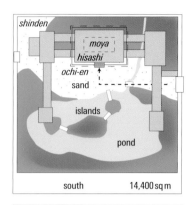

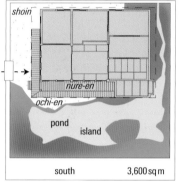

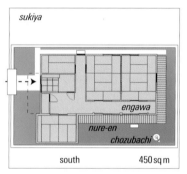

Evolution of building and garden in relation to overall size of the property.

The second great style, *shoin zukuri* was largely the result of removing the outlying buildings of the *shinden*, closing off the main entrance to the building through the garden (placing the garden to the side or back of the building), reducing and externalizing the *hisashi* (corridor), replacing the *shitomido* hanging doors with sliding *mairado* doors, and introducing the idea of fully *tatami*-matted, wall-enclosed rooms. In terms of the garden, the panoramic view was broken down into smaller pieces by the *mairado*, and design focused on controlling the view from seating points inside individual rooms. The pond was nominally retained but overall garden area was greatly reduced. Perhaps more critically, the large, flat, sand-covered area between the pond and building disappeared, or—as with many Zen Buddhist monks' quarters—became a garden in and of itself. Thus the garden came much closer to the interior and the concept of the garden as unenterable art was born.

I began this discussion by pointing to three distinct architectural styles, but there are two other styles critical to the development of both architecture and garden in Japan. These are the *machiya* (townhouse) style and the *soan* (teahouse) style of architecture. The *machiya* style, which grew up in the late Medieval and early Pre-modern eras, actually refers to a number of urban styles. However, most of these are marked by a building—usually a shop—fronting on a thoroughfare and extending back from it to form a residence in the rear. This type of building is usually closely surrounded by similar buildings on both sides, and is contained in a $1/32$-*cho* space (538 square yards/450 sq m) or less. In such an environment, gardens literally turned inward to the interior of the house. Thus the *tsubo niwa*—which was a minor part of both *shinden*- and *shoin*-style architecture—begins to play a major role as an oasis for the new urban dweller.

The second of these architectural developments, the *soan*, or rustic teahouse, was designed as a "mountain retreat" in the middle of the city and was actually an outlet for the recreational and cultural needs of the more well to do among the rising commercial class of the late-Medieval era. This mountain retreat image became the basis of the *roji* (tea garden). Both types of garden required a new application of old rules and in so doing became a source of new rules and innovations which had far-reaching effects on garden design from that time on. Among these are the introduction of stepping stones and stone lanterns, the *wabi* aesthetic of mixing splendor and utter simplicity, and an emphasis on Zen spirituality in everyday life.

The teahouse ultimately "merged" with the *shoin* style to produce the *sukiya* style of architecture, the last great indigenous Japanese style. Here again, decreasing scale was an important factor. Economic "democratization" in the Pre-modern and Modern eras produced a widespread need for modest housing for the growing number of urban dwellers. Again the outer *hisashi* and *ochi-en* (step-down porch) were reduced or totally disappeared, and an "interior *hisashi*" called an "*engawa*" appeared. These developments brought the interior and garden into intimate contact. The pond was increasingly forfeited and artificial hills gave way to *hira niwa* (flat gardens). The interior is now fully fitted with *tatami*-matted floors except for the clay-floored kitchen, bathroom, and *engawa*—which, with its grass-paneled, sliding doors, becomes the ultimate meeting point of home and garden.

■ Elaboration and Stagnation

The Pre-modern era, which basically coincides with the transfer of the capital from Kyoto to Edo (present-day Tokyo), was Japan's longest period of political and economic stability. In architecture and in the garden, it was a period of elaboration of existing styles and general stagnation in new developments. One such elaboration, the *kaiyu-shiki teien* (or stroll garden), grew out of the country villas of retired emperors and assorted royalty. In this period, it developed into a true garden type based on the concept of viewing various natural scenes while wandering along a garden path. New gardens built on the estates of wealthy lords were like early theme parks, featuring specific scenes of famous places from throughout Japan and China arrayed around a large pond. Travel outside the country was strictly prohibited and contacts with the outside world were limited during this period. Eventually, such gardens become the basis of the standard-style Japanese park.

Typical *sukiya*-style home with *engawa* and garden.

On the other hand, the ability to travel the highways within Japan in relative safety gave birth to large and frequent religious pilgrimages, and temples competed for visitors partly on the basis of the beauty of their gardens. Cherry and other types of flower viewing became entertainment for the masses during this period.

The tea ceremony too was elaborated, as the successors to the great tea master Sen no Rikyu divided into three distinct schools of tea—Ura Senke, Omote Senke, and Mushanokoji Senke—creating both a culture and an industry based on, as Sen no Rikyu put it, "boiling water to make tea." While it was the *shogun* Tokugawa Ieyasu's (1543–1616) unification of Japan that created this environment, already under Toyotomi Hideyoshi (1536–98) the industry of war was turning toward the utilitarian industries of daily life.

■ The Modern and Postwar Eras

As we have seen, the history of the Japanese garden is related to three basic factors. I have already outlined two of these—changes of scale and changes in architecture. The third factor—local conditions in the Kyoto basin and the widening of the area in which Japanese gardens came to be constructed—becomes most apparent in the Modern and Postwar years. A combination of several factors has contributed to this.

The Modern era coincide with the fall of the shogun and the opening of Japan to the West. This meant drastic change for all aspects of society. In particular, the newly installed Meiji government invited foreign architects and engineers to come to Japan in droves, bringing with them new methods and new technologies. Having seen the proven superiority of foreign technology, the Meiji government was in a hurry to catch up. New demand for Western-style buildings forced Japanese architects and garden designers alike to apply their ancient craft to new situations. Expansion of Western-style learning and book publishing spurred the need for definitions and patterns that could be understood by anyone. New professions, such as that of Landscape Architect, introduced a dependence on technical drawings, schedules, and estimates. Such dependence lead to the parceling out of work to sub-contractors and, ultimately, to a replacement of traditional skills with standard, modern practices. Although the emphasis on "secret" teachings, handed down verbally from master to apprentice was diminished, the apprenticeship system is still a viable way to learn the craft of garden design and construction.

Though Western garden trees and flowers were also imported at this time, they

HISTORICAL ERAS	
Ancient	650–800
Classical	800–1200
Medieval	1200–1600
Pre-modern	1600–1850
Modern	1850–1945
Postwar	1945–

A bonsai of pine in a semi-cascade style.

were at first limited to large estates and newly developed public parks. Examples of trees that came to Japan are the American sycamore (*Amerika fu*), American plane (*Amerika suzukakenoki*), and the flowering dogwood (*hanamisuki*). Most remained in parks and streets, but some, like the dogwood, entered the realm of gardens. Hybrids of East and West sprang up, and residences in particular often boasted both Western and Japanese buildings, and mixed gardens. This new atmosphere of confusion and experimentation was one factor in expanding the variety of trees used for gardens. Another was the high prices for well-trained garden trees and other materials that could not meet expanding demand. Finally, the dominant position of broadleaf evergreen trees, which flourish in the Kyoto region, was further weakened by the proliferation of gardens in areas with difficult site conditions or that were located further north of where these trees naturally flourish. All these factors contributed to the increase and even centrality of deciduous trees in some Japanese gardens for the first time in history.

■ Personal History and Influences

The two most important developments in the Modern and Postwar eras were the birth of gardens using deciduous trees as primary material, and the new-found focus on *kare sansui* dry gardens. As a person who was raised in these periods, I have been strongly influenced by the pioneering work on *zoki-bayashi* (non-garden or deciduous tree gardens) by Jihei Ogawa (known as Ueji), Kenzo Ogata, and Iida Juki, to name a few. While this trend began in the late 1800s, it came to fruition in the Postwar era. In the town where I grew up and where I still live today, weather conditions are a good bit colder and drier than they are in Kyoto. This poses a dilemma for any gardener who holds the traditional Kyoto style as the ideal. But there is more than enough methodology in the pantheon of Japanese gardening to serve even the coldest and driest conditions. One is the use of deciduous trees—which you will find extensively throughout this book—the other is the *kare sansui* dry garden that dates from the earliest period of Japanese garden history.

The evolution of the *kare sansui* from its description in the *Sakuteiki*—"Where stones have been disposed in a waterless part of a *nosuji* (hillside field) it is called a *kare sansu*." (*kare sansui*)—to the flat sand and stone gardens of Medieval-era Zen monasteries, shows the flexibility possible in constructing a Japanese garden. Though the use of stone was always extensive and varied, there is no evidence to suggest the people of the Classical era ever envisioned the "absoluteness" of the Medieval Zen garden. I have always considered such gardens a high point in Japanese philosophy, spiritualism, and design.

One other person who felt this way was Mirei Shigemori (1896–1975) who, in many ways, brought Japanese garden design into the modern age—along with people like sculptor Osamu Noguchi. Unlike Noguchi, however, Shigemori was a scholar of garden design and a practitioner who built hundreds of gardens between the 1930s and 1970s. He was trained as a painter and brought a painterly vision to his garden work. He was also a prolific writer whose books include a nine-volume work on Japanese *ikebana* flower arrangement and a twenty-six-volume work on the history of the Japanese garden. He pioneered the use of concrete, hard-edge shapes, and color, in abstractions of traditional garden forms. For his radical re-evaluation of Japanese garden design he was reviled by many and remains a controversial figure to this day. But he has always been a source of inspiration to me, and a number of themes that appear in my gardens—swirling shapes and *bengara* red mixed with mortar—are influenced by his work.

Three other strong influences on my garden work are my involvement with the art of making tea (*cha no yu*), my practice of the art of flower arrangement (*ikebana*), and my long-standing involvement with bonsai. From the practice of *cha no yu* I learned the meaning of *wabi-sabi*: to patiently strive for perfection, to leave pride and envy behind. From flower arrangement I learned the importance and fleetingness of living things. To spend long hours carefully cutting and arranging flowers that will be dead in a day or two is to concentrate one's effort in the here and now. Bonsai, which I learned at the feet of my grandfather from a young age, has taught me much about the life of trees and the action of soil, water, and air upon them. It has also taught me much about creating naturalness from the unnatural and arranging trees to maximize their intrinsic balance and beauty. All these practices have taught me that that which is made by human hands is imbued with the mind and spirit of its maker. Japanese culture is a culture of restraint. The Japanese garden is a universe created by those who have perpetually disciplined themselves in this art as well as others. From all these traditions I learned that to create a great garden, one must cultivate a great mind and a great spirit.

■ Literary, Religious, and Visual Themes

In order to focus the spirit in a single direction, it is important to work with a set theme. Whether architect, calligrapher, or potter, the designer conjures a vision— what to make, what to use it for—before setting to work. The gardener sketches an image of what sort of garden to make, perhaps choosing themes from nature, such as a mountain stream or a thicket. Sometimes a representation of a place fondly remembered can conjure an image and set a direction. Literary and religious themes were once quite common to the Japanese garden and the various elements of gardens such as stone settings. Any of these themes will help to decide an overall image. But there is no need to be restricted by a theme. Use it flexibly—responding to the actual physical conditions of your garden and of your own needs and desires as the garden takes shape.

Japanese gardeners still live by the overall principles outlined at the very beginning of the *Sakuteiki*. To paraphrase, these are: 1. "According to the natural conditions of the site, design each part of the garden tastefully, recalling how nature would present itself." 2. "Study the work of past masters and, considering the desires of your heart (or the customer's), create a new work, mindful of what has gone before." 3. "Recall the beautiful and famous scenes of nature, and by putting yourself into the work create a garden full of harmony and the feeling of such places."

These guidelines have a clear direction—naturalness, studied tastefulness, and harmony. They also have clear flexibility—consideration of site conditions, current needs and desires, and self-expression. For example, there is a general consensus that geometric forms not be used in the garden. But there are plenty of examples through-out history of their well-considered use. There is also a general consensus that cut and artificially shaped stone is not natural and should not be used. But it is used, and is becoming increasingly common. This is partly a result of economics and scarcity of supplies, and partly an attempt to make gardens that respond to the urban condition.

A *sanzon seki* decorative stone arrangement—symbolizing the Buddha—is still a basic garden arrangement, although the symbolism is lost on many contemporary viewers.

The point of any teaching is to produce a result that is pleasing or even challenging to as many people as possible. Sometimes introducing a note of discord or tension is an effective way of touching the heart. Rules, as they say, are made to be broken. But study, hard work, patience, and mastery of technique are practices that form the basis for understanding the rules in the first place. Ultimately, the ongoing process of a garden should be something with which you are happy to spend your time.

In this book I use real examples from gardens I have designed, constructed, and photographed to cover the key points of garden making in as much detail as the pages allow. It is my hope that the readers will be able to apply Japanese techniques to their own gardens with the help of this book. Ideally, you should be able to make your own garden with your own hands, and have fun doing so. Take my grandfather Yoshio Oguchi, who worked on his garden his entire life, using the services of professional gardeners when necessary. I believe that it is best to accomplish your own garden in your own way, but without some study you will likely end up with a mess. Having toured thousands of gardens across Japan, I can say that the most common flaw seen in amateur gardeners is lack of restraint and consistency. Finally, consider that because gardens are alive, one should design the garden with a thought to what happens after it has been set up. Will you be able to love and care for it, watering it daily, weeding it, and protecting it from insects, as if it were your own child? The attention you give the finished garden usually matters at least as much as the process of designing and building it.

■ Formal Elements and Design Devices

Gardens consist of a limited number of elements, but a large amount of variety within each element (see chart at right).

A number of design devices have been developed over the centuries, which assist the gardener in realizing the type of garden he or she wants to create. The following list outlines some of these formal and abstract devices:

Formal design principles—Many aspects of Japanese garden design rest on the same basic design considerations as any form of design, anywhere in the world. Scale, shape, texture, division of space, use of light and dark, etc., are all considerations: the point is where to place emphasis. One emphasis is on combining objects in groups of threes. For example, large, medium, and small; horizontal, vertical, and diagonal; close, near, and far; formal, semiformal, and informal (*shin, gyo, so*), etc. Arrangements of objects like rocks and trees are often done in triangular form. For example, three stones are commonly arranged with a larger stone in the center and two lower stones to the left and right front of it. This principle should never be so rigidly exercised as to give the impression of artificiality.

Asymmetry—Another idea common to all design but emphasized as a principle underlying all aspects of Japanese garden design—particularly as opposed to the strict symmetry found in some formal Western-style gardens. A method of avoiding the artificiality mentioned above, the idea of asymmetry is strongly linked to the image of "naturalness" in Japanese design.

Consider the enclosure—One irony of Japanese gardens is that they are able to maintain their naturalness by being cut off from the world around them. Setting a "neutral" background with an enclosure that interrupts line of sight outside the garden is the first essential step in creating the garden.

ELEMENTS	VARIETIES
Theme	Themes are more or less infinite. Literary, nature, design, traditional, are all possible design themes. Another word for theme is "idea."
Design	Designs are also more or less infinite. The design is a matter of taking your theme, your site, and all other existing conditions and molding them into a harmonious totality. Some points related to design are listed on this and the following page.
Enclosure, Divider	These consist of an array of stone, mud, wood, and bamboo fences and walls as well as hedges.
Soil	Soils in Japanese gardens tend to be infused with volcanic materials, giving them generally good moisture retention and drainage. Soil can be purchased locally for any type of planting condition. Piling soil to shape the land is one aspect of creating the garden.
Yaku-ishi—utilitarian stonework *Kei-seki (kazari-ishi)*—decorative stonework	Stones in Japanese gardens are mostly granites and schists, but the shapes, sizes, and textures are more or less infinite. Color is also limited to grays and soft tones. Pure white and strong colors are rarely used except in the form of pebbles.
Water basins	Water basins, the vast majority of which are granite, are used in both natural and cut shapes. Stone objects previously used for other purposes are often reused as water basins.
Lanterns	Lantern shapes are seemingly infinite, but the number of types is limited to no more than ten, with pedestal and implanted types by far the most common.
Trees, shrubs, and plants	Broadleaf evergreen trees are most commonly used in both flowering and nonflowering varieties, along with conifers, shaped pines, and a prevalence of shrubs shaped in rounded forms (*tamamono*). Deciduous trees and moss all play important roles in the Japanese garden.
Sand, pebbles, cobbles	Sand is generally granite sand in sizes of between $\frac{1}{8}$ and $\frac{1}{3}$ inches (3 and 7 mm), but other sizes are used for specific areas. Color is generally dull white to dark beige. Pebbles are used extensively in sizes from $\frac{3}{4}$ to 2 inches (20 to 50 mm) and a range of colors. Cobbles are usually between $2\frac{1}{3}$ and 8 inches (60 and 200 mm) and are generally used for paving along with larger stones.

An approach garden (right) and *kare sansui* (above) showing the influence of Shigemori Mirei in the emphasis on form and contrast.

Framing—Since Medieval times, the Japanese garden has been less a place to play in and more a place to view from a position inside the room. For this reason, the garden is often composed like a painting or a stage set—i.e., with the intention of being seen primarily from one side. Related to this is the importance of the framing from inside the room. As far as possible, the gardener should take a hand in the design of the building as it relates to the garden. This idea goes hand-in-hand with the important principle of seeing the house and garden as one unit.

Eliminate the sky—This is related to framing and refers to the traditional Japanese framing, which is low and wide. The sky is shaded out from the scene with roof eaves or screening devices. Japanese gardens are traditionally built on the south side of the building, so the sunlight causes a strong silhouette and glare if the sky is directly visible.

Shakkei—"Borrowed scenery," meaning to work with the landscape outside of but visible from the garden. Such applications typically involve echoing distant shapes inside the garden, or planting trees in such a way that they appear to blend with trees beyond the garden. The goal is to give the effect of harmonizing the garden with its surroundings. These days, unfortunately, it is often a question of blocking—not incorporating—the scenery outside the garden.

Miekakure—"Hide and reveal" involves placing plants in such a way that a person walking through the garden comes upon a scene gradually. This effect is achieved by controlling the view; concealing it from one point and revealing it from another. It applies primarily to gardens that will be walked through.

Fuzei—"Wind feeling." A visual-emotional term with an abstract quality akin to "taste" or "atmosphere." Also called *furyu* and usually related to garden features that give a feeling of the effect of natural forces. For example, a pine that has been shaped to represent years of battering by strong costal winds, or stones covered with moss and a patina of old age.

Ma—Refers to an interval of space, time, etc. In the garden, it generally refers to the "negative" space between things and how to activate that space.

Mitate—Re-seeing an object or idea and reusing it in a new way. In the garden, this usually refers to using a stone object in a way other than originally intended.

Consider how to care for your garden—Perhaps the most important design consideration of all. Or to put it another way, don't build it if you aren't going to maintain it. For friends and guests, viewing your garden may be enough. But for you, the best part of your garden experience should be those times when you are caring for your garden and taking joy in the way it responds to that care.

■ The Layout of This Book

I have approached the gardens in this book from the perspective of a home or building owner interested in making a Japanese garden. I begin with approach and front gardens, as these are usually the first gardens one encounters when entering a home. These are not typically defined Japanese garden types but are physical areas around the building that usually need attention first. I then move on to *tsubo niwa* (courtyard gardens) and *kare sansui* (dry gardens) that might be found in the middle or rear, or anywhere a small space is available in or around the building. From there, I introduce some tea gardens and tree gardens, which are more likely to be part of a backyard garden or part of a larger garden. Next, I highlight the more specific conditions of gardens in interior spaces—again, not a typical Japanese garden classification but one that may be of particular interest to business owners, designers and urban dwellers. Finally, I show some special garden touches and techniques.

Throughout all the chapters I try to show general layouts and the method of developing the garden, before going into one specific aspect in a step-by-step format. I also try to show practical and affordable variations to give a clear idea of the type and the possible application to your home or building. I advise reading the whole book before attempting any one garden, as helpful information is spread throughout.

Approaches, Entrances, and Front Gardens

Cars do not go with the Japanese style. The late twentieth century saw the dawn of Japan's period of high economic growth. It was also the point at which Japanese towns began losing their traditional beauty. Chrysanthemums and morning glories, grown in little spaces under the deep eaves, were replaced by parked cars, while the *mon kaburi* (gate-shading) pine tree was removed to make space for the widening of narrow streets. Still, many families in Japan have the pleasure of opening their front gate and walking through a lovely garden before entering the house. In this chapter, I hope to share this pleasure of a comfortable approach and welcoming front garden with you.

If you must park a car in front of the house, you can divide the driveway and walkway. If there is only one entryway for both the car and pedestrians, you can design the entryway and the exterior of the house to make them look pleasing when the car is not parked. In the case of a business like a restaurant, a road can be attractively paved and a Japanese garden created to welcome your guests. The gardens in this chapter offer a number of possible solutions.

A SOBA RESTAURANT IN A WOODED RETREAT

Nearly twenty years after I first created a tea garden for my friend and neighbor Akio Miyasaka, he decided to renovate his home and open a *soba* (buckwheat noodle) restaurant.

We separated the private functions of his house garden—with children playing and clothes drying in the sun—from the restaurant garden. For the latter, we created a lovely garden for guests to walk through as they enter and leave, and a garden for them to enjoy while they sit and eat.

Together we created a long approach garden out of what had previously been a concrete road and car park. The new stone-paved path descends steeply from the road and curves round in a U-shape to the entrance of the restaurant. The diversity of the rounded stones (*tama-ishi*) gives a lively appearance, especially accentuated by the fall colors of the tree garden through which it passes. The key with pathways like this is to place strong accents at bends in the path, such as a stone lantern (*ishidoro*), a water basin (*chozubachi*), or a stone grouping. Later on in this chapter I will show you how to create a stone pavement like this one and how to make a screen fence (*misu gaki*) like the one that lines this path.

Informal planting and a mix of medium to rugged texture make for a welcoming approach.

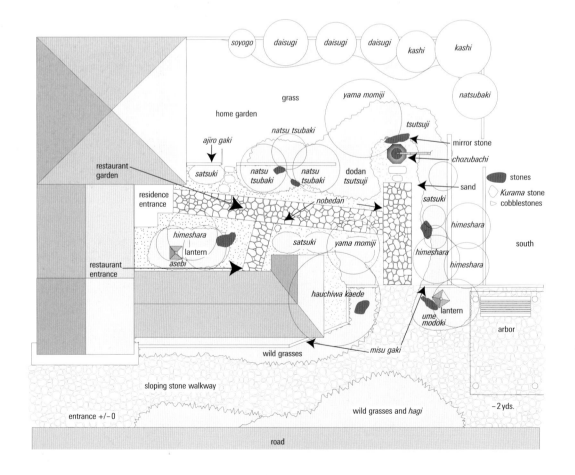

Former life as a drab driveway.

■ THEME, LAYOUT, AND ELEMENTS

Setting the theme of "a *soba* restaurant in a wooded retreat," we created a tree garden (*zoki-bayashi*) of deciduous trees with tea garden accents. As the entrance to the restaurant is far from the main road (33 yards/30 m) and turning in a U-shape, the garden is conceived as a series of paved paths, traveling through a lightly wooded glade. To accomplish this, we used two different paving styles and mostly natural-shaped trees and wild grasses that give the garden a very casual image and a strong seasonal feeling.

Looking at the layout, the entrance from the road to the property was a precipitous concrete slope, previously used as a driveway. We paved this in the *tama-ishijiki* (round stone pavement style), and planted low vegetation on both sides. We concealed the back of the restaurant with a *misu gaki* bamboo and wood fence and transformed the wooden garage at the bottom of the slope into an arbor. A stone lantern is set to mark the point where the slope levels out and turns to the left. Here we made an open entrance gate and changed the pavement to an informal style (*so*) stone walkway (*nobedan*), lined with *Shirakawa* sand. Though the walkway is informal, it actually appears somewhat formal compared to the rough surface of the slope. We decided to line the *nobedan* with *tamamono* (round-shaped) shrubs, used sparingly, with just a few large topiaries of evergreen azalea (*satsuki*). At the end of the first *nobedan* we placed a *chozubachi* and large mirror stone (*kagami-ishi*) in a kind of cul-de-sac. This added depth and an interesting view to what is, otherwise, just the midway point to the restaurant. Before one reaches this corner, another *nobedan* branches off to the left. This leads to the entrance of the residence after

[Layout diagram labels]

soyogo · daisugi · daisugi · daisugi · kashi · kashi

natsubaki

grass

yama momiji

home garden

tsutsuji

ajiro gaki

natsu tsubaki

mirror stone

chozubachi

restaurant garden

satsuki

natsu tsubaki · natsu tsubaki

dodan tsutsuji

sand

satsuki

stones

Kurama stone

cobblestones

residence entrance

nobedan

himeshara

himeshara

south

restaurant entrance

himeshara

lantern

asebi

satsuki · yama momiji

himeshara

hauchiwa kaede

lantern

ume modoki

arbor

wild grasses

misu gaki

sloping stone walkway

– 2 yds.

entrance +/– 0

wild grasses and *hagi*

road

branching off once again to the restaurant entrance. A plaited-mat fence (*ajiro gaki*) on the right side of the pathway blocks the view of the household garden from the restaurant. In the space between the *nobedan* and the building lying in front of the main dining area, I created a small arrangement of mounded earth, plants, and trees; the focal point is a second stone lantern.

Cobblestone walkway.

Elements

The main element in this garden is the pavement stone. To make the journey through the garden more enjoyable, I combined river and mountain stones, in stronger than usual colors, and *Kurama-ishi*—a more classic pavement stone from Mt. Kurama in Kyoto—for the *nobedan*. After the leaves have fallen and been swept away, a good bit of the garden's texture and color is derived from the stone. In the fall, the texture and color of leaves and stone together is especially wonderful.

The garden has been planted primarily with deciduous trees. In particular, *Acer matsumurae* (*yama momiji*), full moon maple (*Acer japonicum*; *hauchiwa kaede*), *Stewartia pseudo-camellia* (*natsu tsubaki*), and *Stewartia monadelpha* (*himeshara*). These trees loose their leaves in winter, allowing sunshine to reach the house. This is especially important for cold regions. Bright green buds in spring, deep green leaves in summer, red and yellow leaves in fall, and the atmosphere created by white snow on dark branches in winter, present the four seasons in all their glory.

Deciduous trees.

The water basin (*chozubachi*) used in this garden is made in the image of the middle part (*chudai*) of a stone lantern. The beautiful rust-colored patina on the stone is probably the result of iron in the water. A large *kagami-ishi* of blue schist (*ao-ishi*) from Shikoku is used to strengthen this setting.

Of the two stone lanterns used in the garden, the one at the base of the slope is an *Oribe* style with a square light box (*hibukuro*) and square openings on all sides. It is a reproduction of the oldest *Oribe* lantern, located in the Myohoji temple of Kyoto. The one in front of the restaurant is also an inserted (*ikekomi*) style, in this case a reproduction of one in Katsura Rikyu in Kyoto.

Kurama-ishi nobedan.

Two bamboo fences are used in this garden: the bamboo curtain (*misu gaki*) style, and the plaited bamboo (*ajiro gaki*) style. The former provides a delicate entrance that perfectly complements the rustic image of the approach. The latter provides a more formal and solid separation between the public space of the restaurant and the private space of the residence.

Oribe stone lantern.

Ajiro gaki.

Misu gaki.

The sloped entrance pavement.

Autumn leaves enliven the *nobedan*.

Transition and texture: *Kurama-ishi*, sand, *tamamono*. A bamboo *ajiro gaki* separates public from private space.

CREATING THE GARDEN

As with most gardens, we start working from the point furthest from the entrance to the property. This is to insure that materials and equipment can enter the site without disturbing completed work. In our case, the first task was to split the private and public garden spaces by constructing a plaited bamboo fence to separate them. Once the fence is in place the actual space of the garden becomes clearer. Next, the ground is leveled and the length, width, and position of the *nobedan*, trees, and plantings, as well as the location of other major elements, can be marked on the ground with lime.

Next, we dig the ground where trees will be placed and plant them. Evergreens like pine or yew are often used in the classic Japanese-style garden, but we chose trees that shed their leaves in winter. Since the garden is on the south side of the house, evergreen trees would block the sunlight, making the house chilly in winter.

We use any excess soil from digging the holes for the trees to create slight mounds along the sides of the paths. Any heavy lifting should be done while it is still possible to bring in cranes, trucks, or other necessary equipment. All the stonework other than the pavement is completed at this point, including the *ishidoro*, stone settings, and *chozubachi*.

In Nagano Prefecture, where the owner and I live, the temperature falls to minus 10 degrees Celsius for at least two weeks every year. This means paving stones can quickly come loose unless the foundation work, consisting of rough gravel, concrete, and reinforcing steel, is properly done. Therefore we dig the ground about 12 inches (30 cm) and lay in a bed of rough gravel and a grid of steel rebar, then pour concrete wherever paving stones are to be fixed.

We begin constructing the *nobedan* from the entrance to the house and restaurant. For beginners, constructing a frame of wood is a helpful guide when constructing a *nobedan*, but level string guides are enough once you have a little experience. I will explain the construction of a semiformal *nobedan* later in this book. The longer the stone pavement, the more attractive it is; 10 yards (9.1 m) is better than 5 yards (4.5 m).

With the azaleas planted and the sand laid in around the *nobedan*, the inner garden area is complete. The next step is to construct the sloped approach. This is detailed in the following section. The entrance gate and arbor are constructed last.

A view of the *chozubachi* and mirror stone from the garden entrance.

The garden takes on a different charm in the snow.

View from the main dining area.

CONSTRUCTING A STONE WALKWAY

Before starting any work on the garden, you need to check the floor level inside the house (FL) in relation to the ground level outside the house (GL). If the floor level is low in relation to the ground outside, runoff from rainwater will be a problem. In the first illustration on the left, the approach slopes toward the house and adequate provision must be taken to insure that runoff will be safely channeled away. Concrete drainage ditches, perforated PVC pipes, or just gravel drainage ditches (French drain) can be used at the bottom and sides of slopes to carry rainwater away. In addition, the ground immediately surrounding the house should be gently graded toward the garden (a 1 to 2% grade). In the case of the Akishino Noodle shop, the sharply sloped part of the approach ends away from the restaurant at the arbor. Without proper drainage this area would become flooded in the rain, rendering it useless as a shelter.

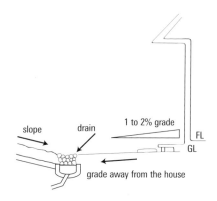

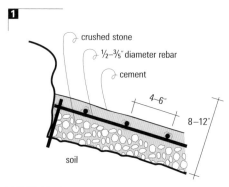

1. In making this or any walkway, the first consideration is whether or not the ground freezes in winter. If it does, follow these steps before laying the paving stone:

   - Dig the soil 8 to 12 inches (20 to 30 cm) deep and keep it aside for creating hills or for leveling other areas of the garden.

   - Put in a layer of round or crushed stone as a base for the concrete.

   - Make a mesh from ½ to ⅗-inch (12 to 15-mm) diameter rebar at a pitch of about 4 to 6 inches (10 to 15 cm). Tie the rebar together with wire to make the mesh and let it sit just above the stone base layer.

   - Pour the concrete to cover the rebar and smooth it, leaving enough space to set your stones above that and have the final surface ¾ to 1 ¼ inches (2 to 3 cm) above the surrounding ground level when finished.

2. Next you will choose and sort your stones. For this walkway we used a colorful mix of mountain and river stones, including black, brown, red, and blue, varying in size from about 2 ⅓ to 8 inches (6 to 20 cm). Each stone should be relatively flat on one side and the shape should be neither too odd nor too geometric. The flat side will be used as the path surface. Each stone will need to be washed to remove dirt that will otherwise inhibit adhesion to the mortar needed to set it in place. A stiff horsehair brush or a brass wire or stainless wire brush is good for this.

3. Make a mortar of three to five parts fine sand and one part cement. Add just enough water to make the components mix well and give you a material wet enough to manipulate but not so wet that the stones will sink into it. The consistency should be such that no water comes out of the material when you squeeze a handful.

4. When placing your stones, try to think in terms of threes. In other words, the overall pattern should contain mostly "Y" and "T" joints but no "+" joints where four stones come together to form a cross. Also try to avoid

long stretches of rather straight joints like a gently flowing river. A joint should end quickly at the face or corner of another stone. Set a section in a bed of dry sand for practice and take a picture—this can help give an overall perspective of the design. Before starting the real thing, drive stakes at both ends of the path and pull a guide string across them to set your finished height.

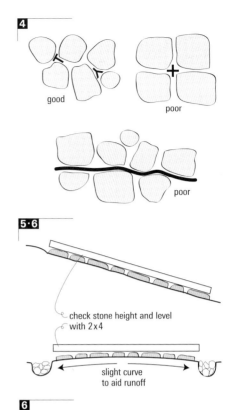

good

poor

poor

5. Put in a small section of mortar and rap the stones down into it using the handle end of a small sledge hammer, allowing the mortar to fill the joints between the stones to a depth of about ¾ to 1¼ inches (2 to 3 cm) from the surface. This will leave room for a final finish to the joint later on. Use a ¾ to 1¼-inch (2 to 3-cm) length of wood to keep checking the depth of the joint. Use a straight length of wood to check that the stones are all at about the same height. The joints should normally be about ¾ to 1¼ inches (2 to 3 cm) wide. Too tight and the mortar between will easily crack; too wide and the road becomes too rough to walk on. In this case, we used a fairly wide joint and irregular placement and a mix of smooth and jagged stones. As the walkway was quite steep we made it a bit rougher than usual to increase traction.

check stone height and level with 2 x 4

slight curve to aid runoff

6. Work from the bottom of the slope to the top and from the center of the path out. Make sure that the path is slightly curved across the width, being higher in the center and sloping toward the edges. This will insure good drainage. Keep stepping back and checking the work from different angles.

7. Finish the joints with a material that fits your image. In this case we filled the joints with a mix of red clay and sand, commonly called *yamazuna* in Japan, and planted moss that we collected from the surrounding area. Using moss that is native to the area is one way to minimize problems. Other possibilities for the joints are sand, fine grass, or mortar.

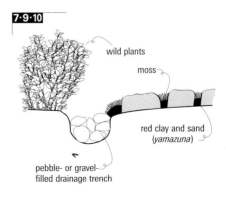

8. When the stonework was finished and left for a day or two to set, we started on the *misu gaki* bamboo fence that hides the building to the left side of the path and creates an entrance to the "inner" garden. This fence will be discussed in detail a little later on.

9. Next, we filled in the soil along the sides of the stone path. We used a mix of black soil and leafy soil (*fuyodo*). After that, we went back and dug a narrow trench about 8 inches (20 cm) wide and down to the top of the concrete under-pavement. We filled this with rounded stone (*goro-ishi*) to create drainage for the water rushing down the slope. This prevents the soil around the walkway from eroding as well.

10. Finally, we planted *Sasa veitchii* (*kumazasa*), wild mountain plants (*yamakusa*) including some wild flowers, and various plants scavenged from along a nearby river. To this I added some bush clover (*hagi*) and some azalea (*satsuki*) around the base of the stone lantern and stone arrangement near the bottom of the slope.

wild plants

moss

red clay and sand (*yamazuna*)

pebble- or gravel-filled drainage trench

Misu gaki: sloped and straight sections. A hint of delicacy in a rugged-looking approach.

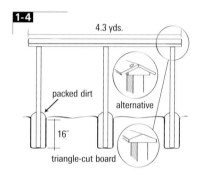

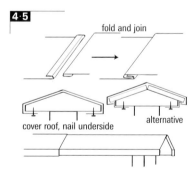

■ CONSTRUCTING A *MISU GAKI* BAMBOO FENCE

1. The *misu gaki* is so named because of its resemblance to a bamboo curtain. In this case, we decided to keep it just above eye level (1.6 to 1.7 yards / 1.5 to 1.6 m) and used a long 2.1-yard (2-m) pitch between the posts. With this fence we are after a delicate, elegant, and slightly rustic look befitting a hospitable establishment. If you want to create a taller fence, you will need more lateral support. This fence has two "L" bends that help with the lateral strength and wind resistance.

2. Dig a 12 to 16-inch (30 to 40-cm) hole for a post of between 4 to 6 inches square (10 to 15 cm). You can char the post with a burner to strengthen it against rot. These days, we usually use pressure-treated posts that are quite durable and save on labor. Tamp down the dirt around the posts to hold them in place. Later on we will add cement to the hole.

3. Nail a board about 8 inches x ¾ inch x 4.3 yards (20 cm x 2 cm x 4 m) in length across the top of the poles to secure them and level them. I advise using flooring nails for all the work on this fence.

4. Two key points about this fence are as follows: 1. A stretch of this fence is on a slope, so the top of each post needs to be cut at an angle, and care should be taken so that the angle of the top board, bamboo, and wide boards parallel each other and the slope of the ground. 2. The top board itself should be cut in a triangular shape to form a roof over the fence. I advise getting this precut from the lumberyard rather than trying to do it yourself. Alternatively, it can be constructed out of several pieces.

5. Cut sheets of copper sheeting (the type used for roofing) and wrap them over the roof board and around the sides to the underside to waterproof it. Nail it in on the underside. Follow the pattern in the illustration or something like it. Alternatives to copper are burning the wood, exterior stain, or cedar bark. Each material will give a somewhat different feeling, but the importance of adding a roof to a bamboo fence to extend its life cannot be stressed enough.

6. Lay out your ¾ to 1¼-inch (2 to 3-cm) diameter bamboo pieces (after cutting them to length) side by side on the ground, and drill holes 1 to 2 inches (2.5 to 5 cm) from the ends for the nails. Nailing directly into bamboo will split it. Laying the bamboo side by side on the ground as you drill will help you keep the holes more or less in line.

7. Start to nail each piece of bamboo to the vertical posts side by side from the top down. Begin 2 to 4 inches (5 to 10 cm) from the underside of the roof board, leaving an open space between the roof and the bamboo. This helps lighten the appearance of the fence. Remember that bamboo is not uniform in diameter—one end is narrower than the other—so alternate the wider and narrower ends as you go down the fence.

8. Continue until about 20 inches (50 cm) of bamboo has been nailed in place. Then nail a board about 12 inches x 2.1 yards x ¾ to 1¼ inches (30 cm x 2 m x 2 to 3 cm) to the posts. This board strengthens the fence and adds to its elegance. It can be treated with exterior stain or charred with a gas burner. Continue the bamboo for

another 12 inches (30 cm) and add another board. Continue nailing the bamboo until you are about 4 inches (10 cm) from ground level.

9. Split a 1½ to 2-inch (4 to 5-cm) diameter piece of bamboo and secure it to the horizontal bamboo with thin copper wire or rope at the halfway point between the left and right posts. Nail it onto the horizontal boards as well. This will keep the long, horizontal lengths of bamboo from sagging.

10. Split a 3 to 4-inch (8 to 10-cm) piece of bamboo and drill four or five holes in it. This will be nailed to the posts to cover the ends of the bamboo and the many nail-heads. Put one half on each side of the post and a third cap over the edge.

11. The constant nailing loosens the posts from the concrete if you put it around the posts at the beginning. Once the fence is finished, dig out the dirt around the posts and fill to 1¼ inches (3 cm) from the top with cement. Temporarily support the fence until the cement dries. Use a plumb line to check the verticality. Fill the hole above the cement with dirt.

The horizontal bamboo can be nailed side by side to create a solid fence, or separated by ⅛ to ¼ inch (3 to 6 mm) to give a more open, semitransparent appearance. With separate sections, such as those we have at the entrance to the inner garden, be sure to keep the height of both sides equal. This includes the height of the middle boards. Pull a level, horizontal string across the front side to check on the height during and after construction.

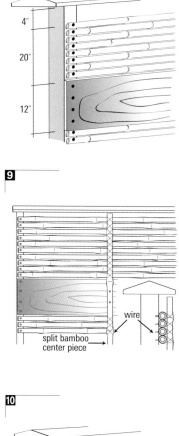

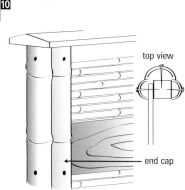

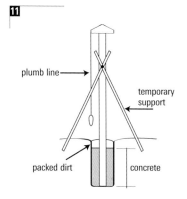

A simple and elegant *misu gaki* frames the entrance and gives the sense of transition from outer to inner garden.

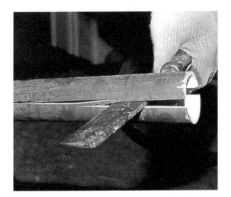

Scrubbed and washed.

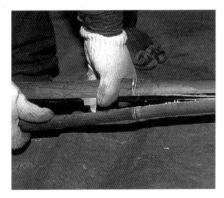

Start split with *nata*.

Keep split centered and pull.

Pull slowly, using your feet and hands.

HOW TO HANDLE BAMBOO

Bamboo is used extensively in Japanese gardens and is thus frequently discussed in this book. Here, I will outline some aspects of bamboo work that apply to most fences and other objects made of bamboo.

Most of the bamboo used for constructing fences is *madake* (giant timber bamboo). This bamboo is very uniform in width from top to bottom and the nodes are far apart, making it easier to keep fence dimensions consistent. The node has a double ridge and the bamboo is available in widths from ¾ to 4¾ inches (2 to 12 cm). *Moso chiku* (*Phyllostachys pubescens*) is also used, but the width from top to bottom varies greatly, making it more difficult to handle. The node has a single ridge with a white band and it is not as strong as *madake*. However, the cost is less and diameters up to 8 inches (20 cm) or more are available. For making a *Katsura gaki*, the branches of *moso chiku* or *ha chiku* (henon bamboo) are best because they have lots of branchlets.

Bamboo grows very fast, reaching its total height in one or two years. But young bamboo should not be used as it is still too wet. Though two-year-old bamboo is sometimes used, three- to four-year-old growth is ideal. The stalks are cut down in the winter to minimize insect infestation and should be used within a year of being cut down. Bamboo that has been sitting in the supplier's storehouse for a long time will have turned yellow, and mold or cracking may be evident.

When handling bamboo, the first thing to remember is to clean it thoroughly. Traditionally, cleaning is done by rubbing the bamboo with rice straw or husks of rice. I usually use a stiff brush and lots of water with a diluted dish-washing liquid. Pay special attention to areas around the nodes, which are particularly dirty. The work is tedious but essential. It can also be done after the fence is assembled, and some suppliers provide bamboo already cleaned.

After the fence is assembled and left to stand for some weeks, the bamboo can be coated with a fungicide, bleach, or a vegetable oil, all of which greatly extend the life of the fence.

■ Cutting Bamboo

Bamboo is commonly used in halves or quarters and therefore must be split. This is done with a *nata*, a hammer, and a lot of brute force. The *nata* is a thick knife with a double bevel. The *nata* is placed at the end of the bamboo in the middle, and rapped with a hammer down through two nodes. Keep this cut as straight as possible. Pull out the *nata*, grasp both halves of the bamboo, and slowly begin to pull it apart. After it gets going, you will find one half getting thinner than the other. Lay the bamboo on the ground with the thinner half down. Pull up the top half while placing one foot on the bottom half. Place your other foot on the top half close to the point where it is not yet split. Use this foot to resist the splitting while pulling on the top half. The quicker it splits, the more likely the split will veer off to one side or the other. As you continue, the upper half will start to get thinner. Turn the bamboo over and continue by pulling on the other half, trying to keep the split centered until the full length is cut. Use the *nata* to remove any shards that appear.

Splitting bamboo is difficult and takes some practice. Another way to approach it is by using a ready-made splitter. Splitters are available to divide bamboo in anywhere from thirds to twelfths, but fence building usually requires no more than fifths. To use the splitter, rap the pointed side down into the end of the bamboo, then grasp both handles and start to pull it down. Rap the opposite end on the ground while pulling on the tool, or put the opposite end against your chest while sitting on the floor and pull the tool toward you. Splitters are easier to control, especially for beginners. Bamboo that is split in halves is often used with the nodes intact, but for quarters the nodes need to be removed with the *nata*, knife, or rasp. Bamboo can also be purchased pre-split.

When cutting across bamboo, use a saw with very fine teeth—a hacksaw is ideal. Bamboo is stringy and tears or splits easily, especially at the end of the cut. Start the cut slowly until you are confident the saw won't jump out of the groove. Cutting a curved and slippery surface like bamboo, especially when cutting at an acute angle, takes practice.

Sometimes it is necessary to remove the nodes in unsplit bamboo, usually for the purpose of passing water through it. Tools are available to do this, or you can just use a length of steel rebar and ram it down through the bamboo. Pulling the rough rebar back and forth through the bamboo is good for cleaning out what remains of the node. On the other hand, there are times when you need to use whole bamboo for fence construction (as with the *yotsume gaki* on page 84). When using bamboo vertically, keep the node as close to the top edge as possible. You don't want water to pool inside the bamboo as this leads to rotting. If it is not possible to keep the node close to the top, fill in the end of the bamboo with a wooden dowel or wax to keep water out.

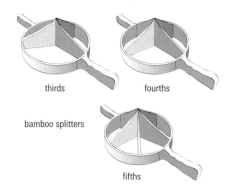

thirds   fourths

bamboo splitters

fifths

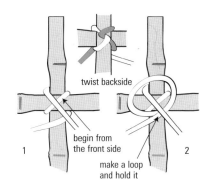

Use the splitter pointed edge down.

■ Nailing and Tying

It is essential to drill a hole for the nail, as direct nailing into bamboo will split it. It is better not to use screws even when drilling first. If the screw gets tighter in the hole as it sinks deeper, it will split the bamboo. Generally, the nailed sides of the bamboo will be covered with a bamboo "cap." In cases where the nailheads are going to be exposed to rain, it is best to use non-rusting nails like stainless, aluminum, or brass. Brass is best especially in cases where the nailhead will be visible (such as the nail for the cap). Again, avoid nailing too tightly against the bamboo as it is easily split.

Tying is traditionally done with *shuronawa* (palm fiber rope) that has been soaked in water to soften it and to cause it to shrink after it has been knotted. Knotting takes lots of practice to get right. These days, even where *shuronawa* is used, the bamboo is usually first secured with copper wire of 1/24 to 1/12 inch (1.5 to 2 mm) diameter. The best wire is called *namashi dosen* (annealed copper wire) and is readily available from bonsai suppliers, as is an aluminum wire with a copper-color surface. This copper wire has been reheated, which makes it softer and easy to twist tightly and snap off cleanly. When the material is not available, taking a bundle of copper wire and "burning" it in a fire produces the same effect but not as consistently—and you must take care not to over-burn the copper.

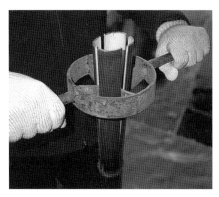

twist backside

begin from the front side

make a loop and hold it

1   2

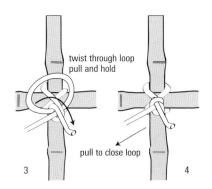

twist through loop pull and hold

pull to close loop

3   4

A MODEST *SUKIYA*-STYLE ENVIRONMENT FOR A *SUKIYA*-STYLE HOUSE

The Nakajima family consulted me from the initial stages of planning the reconstruction of their house. They incorporated some of my ideas and designs into the entire residence, including the parking space and gate. The integration of garden and architecture is a well-accepted concept in Japan, even as economics and expedience have forced the garden into smaller and smaller parts of the property. In Japanese the word *katei* means family or household. The word is made up of the character for *ie* (house 家) and *niwa* (garden 庭), and this is truly the best environment for any

family. Many architects are once again real-izing the importance and attractiveness of this concept by incorporating gardens even in apartment houses.

In planning this house, I made sure that every room would have a view of a garden and that each view would be an effective one. I used all the space from the road to the door, originally intended for the car, to create a clean and bright approach with a trim appearance. I visually expanded the some-what narrow space with a natural continuity that incorporates a low, semitransparent gate. The continuity is maintained after entering the gate, with the amount of green-ery increasing as one approaches the entrance to the house and continues around to the rear.

An old earthen storehouse (*kura*) behind the house was scheduled to be torn down, but I suggested leaving it there as a backdrop to the courtyard garden. I also restored an old well in front of the storehouse to its former beauty, replacing the thirty-year-old pump and curbstones. The whole scene became a picturesque addition to the *sukiya*-style architecture.

A Japanese red pine, Japanese maple, and yulan magnolia that inhabited the old backyard area of the previous house were left in their original places. I added a touch of the Kyoto *sukiya* flavor by planting a vertically branching cedar (*daisugi*) out front. This tree is good in narrow places since the branches grow straight up and leaf only near the top. As with the design of the gate itself, the placement of the footing stones (*tsuka-ishi*) and railing stones for the sliding gate doors—as well as their positions relative to the pavement before and beyond them—was chosen to maximize the beauty and charm from a garden aesthetic. The house, garden, gate, fence, *nobedan*, trees, sand-covered areas, and moss-covered areas should all be well proportioned, clean, and modest—this is the essence of Japanese beauty.

Historically, a roofed gate (*mon*) was a symbol of wealth or status. This photo shows our simple but stately version (with the sliding doors removed).

The house and garden under construction.

■ THEME, LAYOUT, AND ELEMENTS

The theme of this garden is "a *sukiya*-style environment for a *sukiya*-style house." I felt it was important that the house and garden were integrated so they could interact with each other. The environment surrounding the house consists of three main parts:

- The approach garden starts from the road that slants along the lower right edge of the property when looking toward the house. The house is elevated above the road and the approach slopes up to the level of the house. It then levels off just in front of the main gate and continues to the entrance on the right side of the house. The garden is visible until it turns around the house and continues out of sight to the courtyard garden.

- The courtyard garden is to the left of the building when looking from the road. This garden lies between the main building and the restored storehouse in the back. The interior of the house is constructed so that this garden can be glimpsed from the front entrance.

- The main garden on the south side is at the front of the house looking from the road. The Japanese-style living room (*zashiki*) looks out on this garden, which is elevated to the level of the house (about 2.1 yards / 2 m higher than the road). The right side is sloped down to the road and planted with azalea.

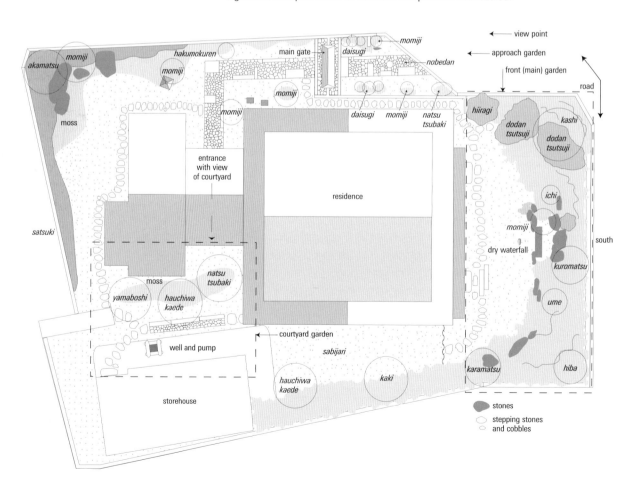

The approach is intended to set a tone of modesty and informality. A *gyo*-style (semiformal) *nobedan* pavement begins from the road and leads to the gate at the top of the slope, continues through the gate, and turns left to the front door. The large proportion of sand in this garden provides a clean and bright, dry landscape (*kare sansui*) style with the planted area increasing as one walks to the house. Finally, the stone lantern slightly enveloped by a large azalea subtly indicates a more restricted area.

Gyo-style *nobedan*.

Materials are carefully selected to fit comfortably with the house and act as an interface with the garden. The base of the wall to the left of the approach is surfaced with the same granite used in the *nobedan*. It is topped with an *ajiro gaki* plaited bamboo fence that adds warmth and provides an appropriate backdrop for the area of the garden behind it as well. The block wall on the right side is steeped down and surfaced with the same material as the house, then topped with Japanese roofing tiles (*kawara*).

Some of the trees in the approach, yulan magnolia (*haku mokuren*) inside the gate, Japanese red pine (*akamatsu*), and Japanese maple (*momiji*) in the back, were part of the backyard of the previous house. The *momiji*, *daisugi*, and Stewartia pseudo-camellia (*natsu tsubaki*) in the front part of the approach were added.

Simple *mon* and lattice sliding doors.

The gate itself is placed at a point where the ground can be leveled and where it will look best from the roadside. It is solid and stately but modest, and the shape is designed to complement the wood framing of the windows and corners of the house. The latticework sliding doors are light and airy.

Between the old storehouse and the residence is a tree-style courtyard garden (*tsubo niwa*) including Japanese dogwood (*yamaboshi*), full moon maple (*hauchiwa kaede*), and others, with a *nobedan* in a semiformal style. But the real feature of this garden is the restored wellhead and pump, and the old storehouse behind it.

The main garden facing the living space is a traditional dry garden (*kare sansui*) that contains a large dry waterfall (*kare taki*), stone bridge, and Buddhist triad (*sanzon seki*) setting constructed with some of the andesite stones (*anzangan*) excavated from the site. Very large stone settings even in small gardens were a popular feature in Japan between the 1960s and 80s.

Old well and new pump.

Elements

The semiformal- (*gyo*-) style *nobedan* is the prominent feature of the approach. The construction of this *nobedan* and the stonework for the gate are detailed following the next section.

The gate (*mon*) is typical of a medium-size gate made for a middle-class family that keeps a somewhat traditional style. These days most houses in Japan are a hybrid of Western and Japanese styles, and where traditional style is still employed, it is usually a stripped-down version. Typical of the hybrid style, many homeowners have incorporated shutters for their car to enter and exit, alongside a traditional, roofed gate.

A dry-waterfall stone setting is the prominent element in the main garden in front of the Japanese-style living room. The mountainous scene behind this garden is borrowed (*shakkei*), adding an echo to the powerful arrangement in the foreground.

Dry waterfall and bridge stone setting.

As with all the gardens in this book, the planning of what parts of the garden to work on first, second, etc., necessarily relies on a number of practical considerations such as budget, the size of the crew, the availability of materials, the design itself, and the weather. In cases where the house is also being constructed, the building contractor's schedule is a key factor. For a house like this one, with gardens on all sides, work actually progresses simultaneously on many different areas.

Generally speaking, we try to group any work that requires renting a crane. Heavy stones, stone lanterns, stone basins, and large trees are brought in at the same time. The stones for the main garden required a twenty-five-ton crane to lift. Before that, a concrete retaining wall was built, as the front garden needed to be backfilled with soil to bring it to the elevated level of the house. After that, the stones were set and the trees planted. The black pine arranged with the stone setting was reused from the old garden, as were most of the stones.

The outer side of the dirt-filled front garden that faces the approach was sloped down to a lower retaining wall and covered with low azalea bushes cut in a *tama-mono* (rounded) fashion. They rise up to the garden and join with the taller plantings that group around the dry waterfall. The drama created by the powerful stone setting, bushes, and tree-grouping peaks in autumn, then lies dormant under the snow until the following year's seasonal cycle begins. An echo of this "crescendo" finds form in the small stone and the ripple of the raked sand in front of this setting.

When making a stone setting, we begin with a drawing. Try to make a drawing showing at least the front and top (plan). This will give you an idea of the size, shape, and number of stones you will need. At this point you would visit a stone supplier and see what you can obtain. Naturally the stones available will not exactly match your image. Mark the stones you intend to buy with a water-soluble material, giving them numbers that correspond to numbered stones in your drawing. Photograph and measure the stones, and modify your drawing based on the actual stones. Also, be sure to buy extra stones. This preparation will make your work on site go smoother. The same basic procedure applies even when the stones are discovered on site, as they were in this case. The difference with having stones on site is that you are able to catalog your stones first, then make your design based on what you have—filling in where needed with stones from a supplier. In our example here, only the horizontal bridge stone was purchased.

Entrance, before and after.

Reverberations of this powerful setting ripple through the sand and echo in the distant mountains.

ENTRANCE GATE AND A *GYO*-STYLE *NOBEDAN*

Before you begin, if you live in an area where the ground freezes over, you will need to lay a foundation of stone and cement first, as we did previously with the Akishino Noodle Restaurant.

From street side to front door, an inviting approach.

1. In the case of Nakajima-san's house, there was a fairly steep incline from the road to the entrance of the house itself. This slope was one important factor in deciding the point at which to fix the entrance gate. You will want to fix the gate at a point where the walkway comes level. The area beyond the gate must be level as well.

   In addition, we would like the *nobedan* inside the gate to be as long and impressive as possible. The overall proportion we decided was 40 percent outside the gate, 60 percent inside. We graded the slope to a point about 20 inches (50 cm) in front of the proposed gate. This gave us space to create a final step up and to level the ground in front of the gate (a person waiting outside needs a level surface to stand on). To surface this part we will use the same stones as those for the *nobedan* and finish the step with cut edging-stones to create the final step up to the gate level.

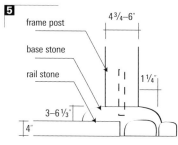

2. Once we decide the position of the gate, we must decide its width. As a rule of thumb for a simple entryway, a gate of no more than 83 inches (210 cm) in width is fine. The doors will be about 43 inches (110 cm) each in width, overlapping each other 4 inches (10 cm) in the center. The doors, frame, and roof of the gate will be made by a carpenter. The stone base will be created and set by us, the gardeners.

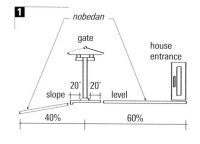

3. Draw lines for the gate with limestone and stick poles in the ground where the posts of the gate will eventually be located. The width of the gate will be your guide in deciding the width of the *nobedan*. As a general rule, one third to one half the width of the gate is a good width for the *nobedan*. However, you want the *nobedan* to have a minimum width of 35 inches (90 cm). If the gate is very narrow, as with tea gardens, consider stepping stones (*tobi-ishi*) or some other surface rather than a *nobedan*.

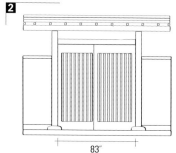

4. The style of the *nobedan* will determine the stones you need. Here we make a semiformal- (*gyo-*) style *nobedan*, which means we need mostly naturally rounded stones, between 2⅓ and 8 inches (6 and 20 cm), and a number of rectangular cut granite slabs of various sizes and proportions. The rounded stones we used are local to the area except for the reddish stones, which were imported from Indonesia. The granite is the same type as we used for the base of the plaited bamboo fence to the left. We also used one round millstone on either side of the entrance. This is a typical *nobedan* arrangement.

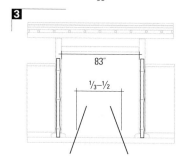

5. A base stone (*sukai-ishi*) of between 3 and 6⅓ inches (7 and 16 cm) height from the finished ground level and 1¼ inch (3 cm) wider than the frame post all around (for a frame post of 4¾ to 6 inches square/12 to 15 cm) will be placed first. The stone is prepared by drilling a hole in the center to accommodate a steel pin of ⅗ to ¾ inch (1.5 to 2 cm) diameter. This will hold the frame to the stone with the help of some epoxy glue. In addition to this hole, the stone will get a cutout to accommodate one of the sliding doors when it is closed all the way to the wood post.

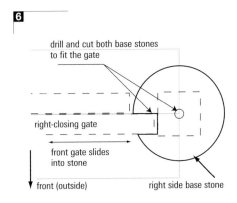

6

drill and cut both base stones
to fit the gate

right-closing gate

front gate slides
into stone

front (outside)

right side base stone

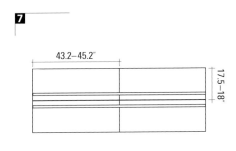

7

43.2–45.2″

17.5–18″

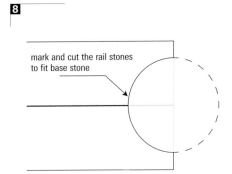

8

mark and cut the rail stones
to fit base stone

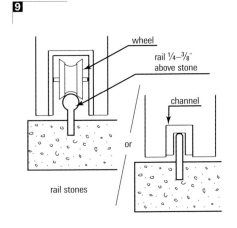

9

wheel

rail ¼–⅜″
above stone

channel

or

rail stones

6. The groove is cut in such a way that the right door will be in the front (outside) and slide open from right to left. The left door in the front is called *hidari mai* and carries the connotation of "bad luck in business" in Japanese. The groove is cut into the same position in both stones and then one stone is reversed. The groove is cut to the depth at which the frame pole will sit, and from top to bottom of the stone. You will need to use a diamond-wheel cutter, small sledgehammer, and chisel for this, or have the work done by a stonemason. At this point, the base stones are set in mortar.

7. Now we will prepare the rail stones for the sliding doors. The rail stone is made up from four cut stones, 4 inches (10 cm) thick and 17.7 inches (45 cm) wide by 43.3 to 45.2 inches (110 to 115 cm) long. These stones will support the metal rails on which the gate doors will ride.

8. We will need to mark cutouts for the base stone (*sukai-ishi*) on the rail stones. First we make a pattern from cardboard based on the shape of the stone. The shape of the base stone is then marked with chalk on the rail stone, then the rail stone is removed and cut out with a diamond-wheel cutter and chisel. After the rail stones are cut, perform a trial assembly with the base stones to be sure they all fit together well. If they don't, re-cut the rail stone, not the base stone. The topside of the base stone is cut smooth and straight to accommodate the wooden post, but the outer sides should remain natural. After you are satisfied with the fit, set the rail stones in a bed of mortar and carefully level everything. This is delicate work that proceeds slowly, but the rail stones must be fitted tight and level.

9. Once this is set, you will cut the grooves for the rails that the doors glide on. This is done with the diamond-wheel cutter. One groove down the center of where each door will glide is cut into the rail stones from one end to the other. The groove is about ⅙ inch (4 mm) deep and ⅛ inch (3 mm) wide to accept the steel or copper rail. If such rails are not available, try using stainless steel flat bars about ⅓ inch (7 mm) tall to fit a stainless or aluminum channel set into the base of the door. Bevel the top edges of the bar, and keep the rail and glide assemblies oiled.

10. At this point the door frame and roof can be brought in and assembled. Once finished, both sides of the gate will be filled with cement block and surfaced. This can be done later but at least before the floor area around the gate is finished. At this point you can check the width of your *nobedan* again and mark the size with string that is tied to stakes in the ground and leveled.

11. We begin working on the *nobedan* from the entrance of the house, again using our string as a guide. The ground has already been dug and a base of cement is laid in. First we will decide which stones to use as the cornerstones (*sumi-ishi*) and set them in mortar. This includes any inside corners as well. Your *nobedan* will look much better, by the way, if you use rectangular cut granite for only one or two of the corners. The

cornerstones should be large enough to be deeply set in the mortar. These stones are most liable to come loose if not properly set.

12. When choosing the cornerstones, it is a good idea to decide the placement of all the large rectangular stones (*ita-ishi*) at the same time. The balance is difficult to master at first. A good way to determine the placement is to make cardboard dummies in the exact size and shape of each rectangular stone you intend to use. Place these within your string lines until you have a satisfying composition. Then set the actual stones in the same place. It is a good idea to get most of the *ita-ishi* set in mortar. Their level can then be used to measure the level of the round stones, and the outside edge preserves the shape in the event the string defining the *nobedan* edge comes loose.

13. Next, start setting the rough, rounded stones. You will need about twice as many stones as the final walkway demands in order to select just the right stones to fit into this puzzle. All the stones will first need to be washed with a brush, to remove dirt and insure adhesion to the mortar. Stack them by the side of your walkway so they will be readily at hand as the work progresses. Lay down cardboard or vinyl first to keep the newly washed stones from getting dirty again. Use these stones only after they have dried.

14. Whenever you decide to end the day's work, cut off the excess mortar that builds up around the outside stones so that you can come back the next day and set new stones as close as you need to. If you leave the mortar until it hardens it becomes difficult to remove. For the same reason, be sure to wash off any mortar from the top surface of the stone before it sets.

15. For the external edges of the *nobedan*, stones with natural corners (*fuchi-ishi*) are chosen. This is slow and difficult work and one reason why it is necessary to have so many extra stones. Since about 1¼ to 1½ inches (3 to 4 cm) of the outside edge will be exposed above the final ground level, mortar will need to be scraped from the outside joints and washed off the visible parts of the stone. Use a straight length of wood to keep checking the straightness of the sides and the level of the *nobedan* stones.

16. The layout of the stones in relation to each other follows the same rules as the previous walkway (see pages 22–23), but don't make the joints too wide.

17. Again, runoff needs to be considered. In this case we used PVC pipes running underground to a manhole, from small round drains placed at points around the *nobedan*. These openings are covered with stainless steel mesh fine enough to keep the sand laid above them from falling through. Consider one drain for 6.5 to 11 square yards (6 to 10 sq m).

18. Wash off the final *nobedan* before the mortar sets. Fill in the joints with *yamazuna* and moss, fine grass, or mortar.

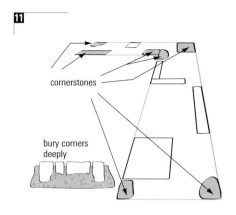

11

cornerstones

bury corners deeply

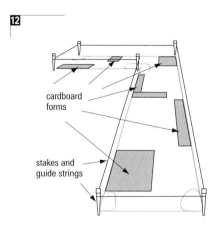

12

cardboard forms

stakes and guide strings

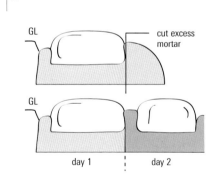

14

GL

cut excess mortar

GL

day 1   day 2

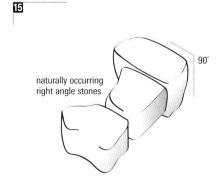

15

naturally occurring right angle stones

90°

Japanese and Western styles in harmony.

Unsightly view of neighbor's house before *Ken'ninji* fence was constructed.

Same view with the fence and inner garden finished.

■ APPROACH AND ENTRANCE VARIATIONS

■ A Street-side Entrance Garden

This large, Western-style house was already standing when I was asked to make the garden. The main question for me was: "How do I harmoniously incorporate a Japanese aesthetic with a Western-modern one?" There are two main aspects to this garden—the inner garden and the street-side entrance.

The inner garden is accessed from the street but is mainly viewed from the Japanese room on the first floor. I played off a literary theme, based on the Chinese legend known in Japanese as *Chikurin no Shichiken* ("The Seven Sages of the Bamboo Grove"). This theme occurred to me because of the large amount of bamboo we intended to use for the fence surrounding this garden. The stone grouping (*iwagumi*) uses seven stones symbolizing the seven wise men. In their midst I placed a slender *nishinoya*-style lantern, a reproduction of a Medieval-era design, chosen by the owner for its smart, vertical profile. A reproduction of a round basin in the Ryoanji temple in Kyoto was chosen to complement it. The markings on this classic basin read: "*Ware tada taru o shiru*," meaning, "I know what it is to be contented (grateful)."

At the back of the garden, a tall bamboo fence was built to conceal the unsightly building facing the first-floor room. I chose the horizontal, split-bamboo *Ken'ninji* style for the fence, owing to a tight budget and the need to conceal the unattractive view. Applying split-bamboo horizontally causes it to deteriorate more rapidly, but this is relatively inexpensive and simple to replace.

The fence facing the street side is made in the same manner, but the upper fourth is crafted into an openwork plaited fence, giving it a lighter feeling. The entrance is made low and left open except for a removable bamboo pole that signals when the entrance is open or closed.

The client owns many cars, so I decided the front area should serve the purpose of parking but retain the appearance of a garden. I paved the area in front of the house with cut granite slabs measuring 15 ¾ by 47 inches (40 by 120 cm), leaving the existing crape myrtle in the middle of the space (far right in the photo at left). I opted for wide grassy joints—about 2 to 3 inches (6 to 8 cm) wide. The grass softens the sharpness of the architecture and the granite, giving it a garden feeling. Some black bamboo was added along the front of the building for the same reason.

Another crape myrtle growing in the back of the property was transplanted to the front-left to complement the Japanese-style fence behind it and create a connection with the trees inside the garden. A legless lantern put together from random stones in the family's possession "grounds" the tree. With Western architecture, planting distinctly Japanese trees—such as shaped pine or ball-pruned, little-leaf boxwood—creates a dissonance. Trees with natural shapes work better with Western-style houses.

■ A Long Approach and Tree Garden

This long approach garden is one of four separate gardens I made for the Ishizone residence (see page 65). I also gave advice on how to make a Western-style building that goes well with Japanese gardens, including such points as fitting large windows in the rooms that look out onto the gardens. The question of how best to balance Western-style architecture with Japanese garden aesthetics is one of the main challenges faced by garden designers today.

The approach was made into a tree garden. No gate was built on the street side, as this is a rural town with little concern about security. Only a sleeve fence (*sode gaki*) was installed to visually separate the garden from the street. The gateway in the photo below is at the back of the approach—at the entrance to the garden of the residence. The walkway is made of diamond-shaped stepping stones, set in a straight line into a base of *araidashi* (exposed aggregate), and surrounded by sand.

This garden is in a town close to the Japan Alps, and the autumn leaves in this region are particularly striking. The trees were therefore chosen primarily for their autumn foliage: Japanese maple (*iroha momiji*), *Sorbus commixta* (*nanakamado*), Japanese hornbeam (*kumashide*), Japanese dogwood (*yamaboshi*), *Dendropanax trifidus* (*kakuremino*), full moon maple (*hauchiwa kaede*), and the evergreens *Quercus myrsinaefolia* (*shirakashi*), *daisugi*, and *satsuki* and *tsutsuji* (both azaleas). When the garden is narrow, it is best to choose trees that do not have lower branches. But this leaves the unsightly parts of the neighbor's property in plain view, so we obtained the neighbor's consent to paint the wall of their building white and construct the bottom part to give the appearance of an earthen wall topped with roof tiles. Many visitors came to appreciate the garden in the fall following its completion, and this appreciation has continued for many years.

The gate at the end of the approach is within the property, so it has been fitted with modest doors and given an unimposing appearance. Strength is added to the slender doors by attaching crosspieces (*san*) in a random diagonal (*fukiyose goshi*) design.

▶ Inner gate to *kare sansui* garden.

Long approach in autumn color.

Previous appearance.

The revitalized entrance to Jiunji.

Before renovation: dark and heavy.

Under the trees: reflected light and definition.

Elements of relief and rest.

■ Reviving a Dreary Entrance

The residence of the chief priest of the Jiunji temple is a *sukiya*-style structure, and a ready-made wooden gate stands in front of it. The client's request was to improve the look of the approach without changing the gate. As the approach stood, it was dark and foreboding, and the magnificent large stepping stones looked badly placed and disjointed. Leaving the gate and large stepping stones as they were, I added haircap moss (*sugigoke*) between and around the stones. This added some color and gave them a more harmonious appearance. A ⅕-inch (5-mm) diameter *sabi jari* (rust-colored granite gravel) was laid over what had previously been only black earth. Lots of exposed earth, especially under trees, creates a dank atmosphere. This color of gravel sand adds light and cleanliness and just enough contrast to better distinguish the shape of the garden. We also remade the passage that branches off to the right toward the annex and—without moving the large stones and trees—planted Japanese maple, Japanese storax (*eigonoki*), Japanese dogwood, and Stewartia (*natsu tsubaki*). This added some verticality and delicacy that further enlivened the dreary mood.

In order to make a garden that maintained a serious air but has vitality and variation, paving stones were laid along with stepping stones, and an *Oribe* lantern and a *shiho-Butsu* (four-Buddhas) water basin was added at the far end of the garden under the trees. The basin is a *mitatemono* (see page 59) originally part of a stone pagoda, hollowed out to make a basin. Jiunji is a good example of how to enliven a garden when it becomes too overgrown and shoddy. I advise strengthening the composition with elements like stone groupings and stone lanterns, lightening and defining the ground plane with sand, and replacing overgrown trees and bushes with narrow-trunk trees and lower, well-shaped bushes. The result is lightness, variety, and stability.

■ A New Entrance Using Old "Stuff"

The client asked me to create a well-proportioned front garden and entrance composition incorporating dissonant items such as an existing aluminum fence and thick granite columns flanking the entrance. This type of granite column became popular in the Modern era. A nameplate is usually affixed in an attempt to imitate the entrances of large estates in Europe. As is so often the case, we are unable or unwilling to throw everything out and start from scratch, thereby being forced to combine what we have with what we hope for. In this case I decided to make two distinct gardens: a front garden for the Japanese room and an entrance garden. Though the space was limited, the characteristics of each garden were drawn out to the furthest extent possible and lightly fenced off from each other.

We started by covering the aluminum fence on the interior side with a split-bamboo fence similar to the *Ken'ninji gaki* previously highlighted in this book. With such a narrow space—about 2 yards (less than 2 m) deep—few trees and no bushes were planted. One large Japanese persimmon (*kaki no ki*) was already there and a *daisugi* was added to this. I opted for a more symbolic garden of sand and paving stone. This surface reflects light into the room while lending an air of quiet contemplation.

Since there are only about ten steps from the road to the front door, an entrance gate was virtually essential but would look pretentious unless it was kept simple and low. Building a low wooden lattice gate with plank walls on both sides (*itabei*) and a thin, shallow-angled roof, achieved a *sukiya*-like gentleness that belies the imposing granite columns outside. While the overall gate composition would certainly look more refined without the large stone columns, they have been left there at the client's request. The wood is stained a dark color to approximate the bronze-tone aluminum fence. This creates a uniform appearance from the outside and adds some dignity to the modest appearance. Furthermore, the new gate allowed the opportunity to make over the gate-shading pine tree (*mon kaburi*) into its rightful shape.

The tiny space from gate to door was kept simple, using only granite stepping stones, moss, bamboo, dwarf bamboo, and sand. As moss will not grow under a roof, it has been planted only where dew and sun will be sufficient. The addition of the gate and fence created an intimate and much-needed buffer zone between the house and the adjacent road. Such a simple solution is open to anyone needing to create a small sanctuary in an urban environment.

From the inside, a peaceful buffer zone.

A symbolic peninsula of stone juts into a swirling ocean of sand.

Uncomfortable bedmates: stone pillars, aluminum fence, Japanese-style architecture.

AN ECONOMIC "WEED" GARDEN FOR THE SAKURA NOODLE RESTAURANT

"I'm opening a *soba* restaurant soon. The building is almost completed, and I would like you to make the front garden," said the new, female owner. "I saw your work on the Akishino Noodle Restaurant, and thought our restaurant should have a garden too."

It is fairly rare in Japan to come across female owners of buckwheat noodle (*soba*) restaurants. This lady, however, was on the verge of realizing her long-cherished dream. Only she hadn't planned for a garden and did not have much money left. So we decided to make a "weed" garden (*zasso*), and kept the cost down by transplanting wild plants from around the nearby rice fields, mixed with trees and flowers from the owner's home garden. Having been informed that the area was once called Sakura (cherry tree), I added three double-flowered cherry trees (*yaezakura*) from my nursery. And as the property was actually part of the adjacent rice field, the owner had the right to draw water from the nearby river, which we used to make a small pond and stream (*yarimizu*).

Though it may hurt my standing in the profession to make "weed" gardens, Sakura's garden is well liked by the restaurant's customers—many of whom are city dwellers. Perhaps because places like Tokyo hardly even have weeds these days, passing a pleasant afternoon eating *soba* among greenery and the sound of a stream is a joy for many people. Of course, those interested only in convenience may complain about a lack of parking. Unfortunately, there are all too many places for people who want to drive in, eat fast, and drive out. A garden slows people down, invites them to breath deeply, and refreshes their spirit even as the food refreshes their bodies.

The owner has a great love for flowering plants, and the garden has become one that she can enjoy working on even after its completion. In traditional Japanese gardens, adding plants or changing anything the gardener has done is discouraged. Even maintenance should be entrusted to a professional—this is the Japanese way. But I encourage my customers to work in their gardens and plant anything they like, with the restriction that ornate flowers like the rose, or exotic plants like the cactus, which are thoroughly Western in nature, not be added. Though Sakura is quite different from a classic Japanese garden, I think any garden that is cared for, loved, and brings pleasure, is good in its own way. In any case, no one ever loved a parking lot.

ABOVE: "Weed" Garden of the Sakura Noodle Restaurant.
LEFT: If it comes to a decision to put in a parking lot or a garden, the choice is obvious if you follow your instincts— as do many customers looking for a relaxing place to eat.

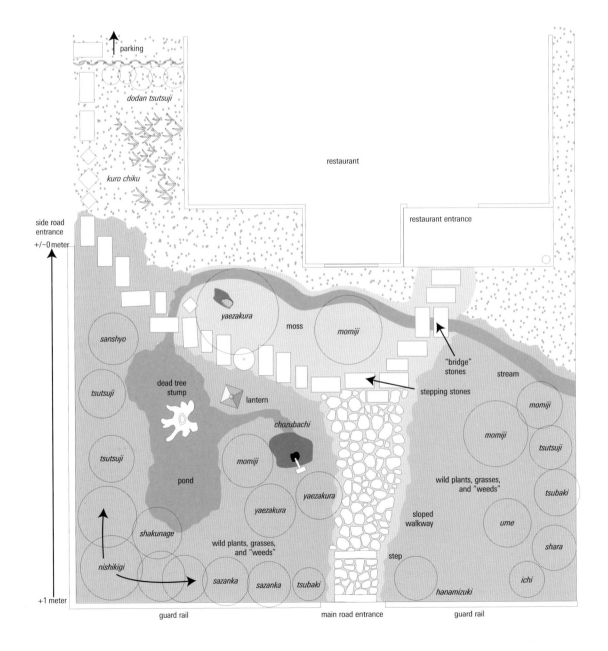

THEME, LAYOUT, AND ELEMENTS

As I mentioned in the opening, the theme of this garden is "a garden of weeds." Accordingly, it has a natural, undesigned, slightly wild feeling—perhaps closer to the idea of a mountain retreat idealized in the tea garden. Yet it does have several features, such as an artificial hill and a stream, common to a classic *tsukiyama*-style garden.

The property for the restaurant was sectioned off from the rice field that now surrounds it on the right and back side (when looking toward the building). The land is lower than the main road that passes on the front side of the property by just over a yard (about 1 m). The road on the left side slopes down to meet the property about halfway through. When I was brought in to do this work, the restaurant had already been located toward the back of the property with the expectation that the front area would be used as a parking lot. This would be accessed from the road on the

Nothing inviting about the location before we went to work.

parking

dodan tsutsuji

kuro chiku

restaurant

restaurant entrance

side road entrance
+/−0 meter

yaezakura

moss

momiji

sanshyo

"bridge" stones

stream

tsutsuji

dead tree stump

lantern

stepping stones

momiji

momiji

tsutsuji

chozubachi

momiji

tsubaki

tsutsuji

yaezakura

wild plants, grasses, and "weeds"

pond

yaezakura

ume

shara

shakunage

sloped walkway

nishikigi

wild plants, grasses, and "weeds"

step

ichi

+1 meter

sazanka

sazanka

tsubaki

hanamizuki

guard rail

main road entrance

guard rail

left. The concrete wall on the front and lower left corner, plus the steel pipe fence along the main road, made for a very unnatural and unsightly backdrop to the garden. Sometimes, when the shape of a plot for the garden cannot be changed and ugly backgrounds would require building huge fences, changing land elevations can create the proper atmosphere of intimacy needed for a Japanese garden. I decided to create an elevated entrance on the front side that appeared to set the restaurant in a natural-looking valley. To do this required piling soil to the level of the main road and removing a section of the metal railing.

Once this plan was set, the other elements fell into place. It would be necessary to create several steps down from the main road. Some parking would be retained toward the left rear of the restaurant, and this naturally dictated stepping stones coming around from the left to meet the path from the central entrance. The stepping stones terminate further right at the restaurant entrance. I used granite slabs for stepping stones to add contrast to the garden and because they are cheaper than good-quality stepping stones.

Though we had an ample source of water, the garden was too small for a large pond and the budget prohibited it. I decided on a very small pond and a meandering stream that snaked through the garden and crossed the path in two places. This gave the water feature an understated prominence without requiring much space or money to build. One year after the opening, I was able to convince the owner to invest in a boat-landing (*funa tsuki*) lantern—modeled after the original in Katsura Rikyu—and I placed it at a key junction in the garden to create a strong focal point.

Low lights illuminate the way for evening guests. While lighting up the entire garden from the eaves suits design-oriented gardens and Western-style flower gardens, Japanese gardens look best with low path lamps (*roji andon*). Not only should lights be used low, but they should also be used sparingly, to maintain a quiet and natural atmosphere and the feeling of mystery that comes when everything is not starkly revealed.

Elements

Though the theme is "weed garden," mounded earth is actually the main element of this garden. Even more "silent" than stone, mounded earth is a key player in traditional Japanese gardens.

Water as an element in this garden takes the form of a meandering stream that seems to have its origin from a water basin (*chozubachi*), strategically placed halfway up the left side of the artificial mountain, when entering from the main road. The *chozubachi* is just a rough stone with a natural hollow that suggests a basin.

The cherry trees, which are the namesake of the restaurant, are prominent in spring—when they burst into bloom for a brief time. In that short period they become the main element of the garden.

For most of the year, the weeds, wild plants, and seasonal grasses, along with a few deciduous trees, are the main elements.

The *funa tsuki* lantern is also a prominent feature of the garden, particularly in the snowfall. At that time, the combination of lantern and stream is an absolute delight.

The lighting is an important element of the garden at night. Real Japanese *roji andon* were beyond our budget, so we cut the posts of pedestal lamps and converted them into low path lights.

The stream emerges from the stone *chozubachi*.

Reflecting the restaurant's name, cherry trees provide the atmosphere in spring.

A wild and natural looking "weed" garden.

The stone lantern symbolically lights the stepping stone path.

Piling earth to the height of the road.

Rough layout of stepping stones.

Cherry trees in bloom.

■ MAKING THE "WEED" GARDEN

1. The key point of the design was building up the ground to create an entranceway and intimate "valley." This corner property had a drop from the road on one side of about 1 yard (1 m) and a railing—owned by the city—enclosed the property on that side. In order to fulfill our plan, we first had to get permission from the city to remove a 2.1-yard (2-m) section of the railing at approximately the front center of the property.

2. Next, we needed to build up the ground on the same side in order to create the entrance path. For this we used about 20 tons of 80 parts black soil to 20 parts *yamazuna*, mixed thoroughly on site. This was mounded like a hill toward the section of the fence to be removed.

3. The next step was to lay out the *tobi-ishi* according to our plan and our judgment on site. For *tobi-ishi* we used cut granite, about 4 inches (10 cm) thick and various sizes. Aside from being cheaper than natural stepping stones, the granite slabs provide an easy and safe surface to walk on for children and the elderly. They also add an element of "hardness" in an otherwise "soft" garden. Once the stones are roughly laid out, we mark their place with limestone and remove them to plant the trees.

4. We planted three *yaezakura* cherry trees to complement the noodle shop's name. One reason for planting big trees early on in creating the garden is that the soil removed for the root bundle can still be used at this stage to shape other areas.

5. Because the property was previously used for rice farming, we had the right to draw water from the nearby stream. As the garden area is small, we made a very small pond and stream that churned in a twisted route and deposited its water into the rice field next door, used by the same owner. Long ago, when the "ideal" south garden with a large pond was imported from China, it often became modified into a stream to suit the smaller plots allotted to Japanese aristocrats. Necessity is truly the mother of invention.

6. As the cost of concrete or even vinyl liner was too high, we just dug out the pond and stream with a backhoe—the pond to a depth of 12 inches (30 cm), the stream only 3 inches (7 cm) deep. Weed and silt buildup need to be kept in check, but otherwise no problems have occurred. This stream shows that, craft and tradition aside, sometimes simple alternatives are fine.

7. The water is pumped from the stream on the opposite side of the road—through a viaduct originally used for this purpose—using a typical garden hose buried to a depth of about 4 inches (10 cm) and a small 200-volt pump submerged in the stream. It terminates at a water spout (*kakehi*) arrangement that is constructed as follows:

   • Cut a block of wood about 3½ inches (9 cm) square and 8 inches (20 cm) long. Cut a hole in the center of the bottom about 1½ inches

The meandering stream enlivens the atmosphere with sounds and reflections.

(4 cm) in diameter halfway through the block and another of 1 inch (2.5 cm) in the side in such a way that they meet in the center.

- Take a length of bamboo with a diameter that can fit into the bottom hole and use a steel pipe to knock out all the nodes. Fit this into the hole in the wood block. Take another shorter length of bamboo to fit the second hole and knock out the nodes in this one too. Then cut one end of this bamboo at a slight angle and fit the bamboo into the side hole so that the cut end is outside. Run the hose up through the bottom bamboo as far as it will go and stick the whole assembly securely into the ground, taking care not to crush the hose (cut out a space for it to enter the bamboo from the bottom side).

- It may be a good idea to make a joint where the hose leaves the ground for easy rearrangement or repair in the future. It is also possible to buy ready-made *kakehi* or a kit.

8. The owner had a large stone with a hollowed-out area that we used to let the water cascade into and out of. We set the stone and *kakehi* at the head of the pond about one third of the way up the side of the hill made for the entrance. The overflow formed the source of the pond.

9. Because we now had a meandering stream interrupting our path, we needed bridges to cross it. Again, these were made very simply by placing a stepping stone across two edge stones. The finished bridges look just like any of the other stepping stones because they are placed at the same height and in line with the others. Occasionally, a tipsy customer will miss the stone and step in the stream, but it is too shallow to cause any more harm than a wet shoe.

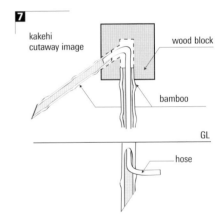

7
kakehi cutaway image

wood block

bamboo

GL

hose

A bridge disguised as a stepping stone (lower right corner).

Laying in stones for walkway and steps.

The completed garden.

Cherry trees are inviting in spring.

10. From the road where the gate was removed, we originally intended just to create a stone walkway (see page 22) but found the slope too steep. We therefore created two elongated, gently sloping steps. Again, due to the lack of money, we used no concrete foundation. As time goes on some stones will move, but they can easily be repaired. Instead, we simply mixed dry cement with the dirt under the intended steps, and tamped it down to form a firm base. The same flat granite as the stepping stones was used for the edge of the stairs, then rough, rounded stones were laid in. The same dirt and cement mix was tamped between the stones as well. Finally, water was sprinkled over the finished area and left to penetrate and harden the cement-dirt mix.

11. Next, we collected our weeds and shrubs from the surrounding fields, and everyone helped in this effort as well as in the planting. To the cherry trees from my nursery I added *sazanka*, *tsubaki*, *yamaboshi*, several *momiji*, *Rhododendron degronianum* (*azuma shakunage*), Japanese enkianthus (*dodan tsutsuji*), black bamboo (*kuro chiku*), and some haircap moss (*sugigoke*) around the walkway stones.

12. Before finishing the planting, we dug a trench 1¼ inch (3 cm) wide and deep from the property entrance to the house for an electric cord. Regulations in many areas will require a metal conduit for this, but if there is no regulation, we find heavy-duty electric cord works just fine when buried in the ground (sunlight is the biggest enemy of rubber-coated cord). For lights, we were restricted by costs to very standard outdoor pole lights. In order to suit a Japanese garden, lighting should be kept close to the ground, so we cut the poles short. Some time after the opening of the shop, a friend of the owner's presented her with the more attractive light shades shown in the photos.

13. One year after the opening, I was still looking for a focal point to give some small formality to the garden. I was able to convince the owner to buy a *funa tsuki-gata* lantern, which suits this garden well. The lantern was placed at the point where the stepping stones, which come in from the parking space at the back of the property, turn left toward the entrance. Even when not used as a functioning light source, the lantern should always be placed as if it were.

▶ TOP: Granite slabs reflect just enough light from the low *roji andon*. BOTTOM: The stream becomes pronounced in the winter and a new image of nature emerges.

CHAPTER

2

Courtyard and
Dry Landscape Gardens

In this chapter, I will present a wide variety of courtyard (*tsubo niwa*) and dry gardens (*kare sansui*). Next to entrance and front gardens, the *tsubo niwa* is perhaps the most applicable to the average home, office, or shop. Small scale and a need to integrate the garden with existing architecture are part of the reason for this. *Kare sansui*, on the other hand, are associated in many people's minds with monks and meditation. But this need not be the case, as I will try to illustrate.

SMALL COURTYARD GARDEN FOR A MODEST HOME

Although this residence was fairly modern, the client wanted a Japanese garden. The two-story house had only one Japanese-style room surfaced with *tatami* (straw mats) on the first floor, as is often the case in Japanese homes and apartments these days. It was decided that just the area in front of the room would be made into a traditional courtyard garden, with the adjacent area to be covered in grass. In order to even think of creating a Japanese garden for this residence, it was first essential to enclose and isolate the area with, in this case, a bamboo fence. Japanese gardens can be costly to make; even small gardens of two or three *tsubo* (7.2 to 10.8 square yards / 6.6 to 9.9 sq m) can cost a startling amount. For this reason, too, it was decided that only the area facing the Japanese room would be made into a Japanese courtyard garden.

Unlike some Western-style architecture, traditional Japanese architecture contains many ambiguous elements that may be considered as part of either the garden or the house, such as a corridor that can open out along the exterior of the house (*engawa*), an open veranda exterior to the house (*nure-en*), shoe-removing stone (*kutsunugi-ishi*), a roof overhanging a hard-packed earthen floor (*dobisashi*), and a curb or walkway (*inubashiri*). Since this house had none of these elements, I proposed building a *nure-en* as a simple way to better integrate the house and the garden.

This garden is primarily intended for appreciation from within the house; in effect, a three-dimensional picture. It was therefore necessary that the courtyard garden of the Kobayashi residence be enclosed in a fairly high bamboo fence to erase from this picture the neighbor's house, a concrete telephone pole, and an ugly—but necessary—metal storage shed.

The type of fence used is a plaited fence (*ajiro gaki*), which is intended to look good from both sides. The section facing the adjacent lawn is an open weave intended to help visually expand the garden and let in light and air. Japanese courtyard gardens often incorporate a stone lantern and water basin derived from the format for the tea garden. We kept this convention for our *tsubo niwa*, which added a touch of formality to an otherwise casual setting.

A classic arrangement of water basin and lantern is dappled in patterned light penetrating the open-weave *ajiro gaki*.

A storage shed, soon to be hidden from view.

THEME, LAYOUT, AND ELEMENTS

This garden proceeded from a design theme which was "to give a good view from the Japanese-style room, and create a pleasant and private outdoor space that brought nature close to the interior." The backyard was just a flat, open space, facing the neighbor's property and an unsightly electric utility pole. The owners had a metal storage shed in this space that they wished to retain. Given these conditions, the first priority was to move the metal storage shed to the very back edge of the property and enclose a space adjacent to the Japanese-style room to create the garden in.

For this enclosure, a rather tall bamboo fence was the best choice. There are several reasons for this. A hedge like the one on the side of the property is better kept for a large space where it has ample room to grow. As we had a limited space of less than 17 ½ square yards (16 sq m), the widening hedge would shrink the space. In addition, the hedge needs regular maintenance, which the owner was against. The other good point about the bamboo fence is that it can be constructed to completely block out the view, to let in some air and light, or any combination of the two. Properly constructed with a roof and treated with a fungicide, well-made bamboo fences will last for fifteen years or more.

One thing I did insist on was to build a *nure-en* to increase the connection between the interior and exterior and to give some feeling to the bare and featureless architecture. Therefore, we constructed a 24-inch (60-cm) wide *nure-en* along the entire back of the house and designed the garden with this feature in mind.

Now, considering that we will construct a bamboo fence, it is best not to pile soil against it to create a change of level. Piling dirt against bamboo will cause it to rot in three years or so. This, plus the limited size, dictated constructing a flat (*hira niwa*) garden. Returning to our theme of a garden giving "a good view from the Japanese-style room," we next consider the elements and their placement in relation to this theme.

The traditional ideal since the Pre-modern era is that the "place of honor," in seating a guest or head of the family, is the position in front of the *tokonoma*—an alcove used for displaying a vertical scroll (*kakuji*) or flower arrangement (*ikebana*). In this

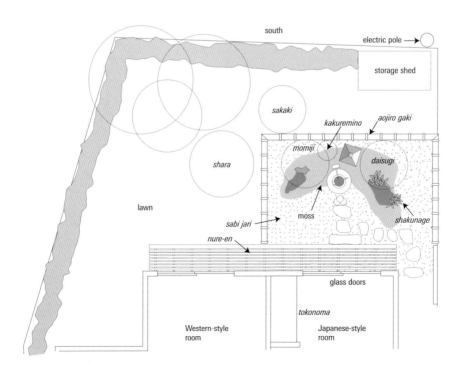

case, it was the left side of the room when facing the garden. So the best view should be from this point. In terms of the elements, again since the mid to late Premodern era, the "archetype" of the Japanese garden has centered on the combination of stone lantern (*ishidoro*), stone basin (*chozubachi*), a stone setting (usually including stepping stones), moss (*koke*), and pine (*matsu*). This group of elements epitomizes what is for everyone in the world—including the Japanese—the quintessential Japanese garden. While this may seem like a shallow stereotype to some, I find that a certain amount of "cultural shorthand" is one means of keeping alive the 1500-year-old tradition of Japanese gardening in a world of "sound bites" and shortened attention spans. Even so, carefully shaped and maintained trees, such as pines, are disappearing from home gardens as preferences change toward flowering and low-maintenance trees.

For plantings, a single Japanese full moon maple (*hauchiwa kaede*) gives a thick canopy of green leaf with a relatively narrow, multiple trunk, and provides a strong sense of seasonal change. To hide the view of the ugly electric pole, a *Cryptomeria japonica* (*daisugi*) is ideal. To complete the setting, I chose a smaller *Dendropanax trifidus* (*kakuremino*)—a broadleaf evergreen that provides leaf at a lower level than the *daisugi*. For planting the haircap moss (*sugigoke*) and pulling the elements together in a cohesive form, some dirt will be piled up in a kind of island. I decided to make this in the shape of a *magatama*, one of the sacred objects of the Japanese Shinto faith, which also happens to be a nice curving, asymmetric shape. A space is left open between the piled earth and the bamboo fence that will keep the bamboo dry and serve visually to increase the depth of the garden.

To walk from the house to the water basin, stepping stones will be needed, as well as a shoe-removing stone (*kutsunugi-ishi*) to step down from the *nure-en* to the garden. Finally, sand will be laid over the better part of the garden to add a low-maintenance finishing touch that will contrast the green of the plantings.

The key to making a fine courtyard garden is to work with few materials and aim for simplicity. If one were to freely plant flowers and trees, in five or ten years the garden will look like a nursery, or worse yet, a dump. Even if you are tempted to plant various species, it is essential that you restrain yourself and use only the minimum number of fine materials appropriate to the theme of your garden. Leave the remainder as blank or negative space. Seeing and feeling the tension between positive and negative space is an essential requirement in creating your Japanese garden.

Elements

The stone lantern is an *Oribe* style (also sometimes called a *hina-gata* or Christian lantern) with a rectangular base and square light box.

The water basin is in the form of a *soban* (footing stone for pillars). Stone objects are often used in the Japanese garden in ways other than the originally intended purpose.

The plantings are full moon maple, cedar, *kakuremino*, haircap moss, and *shakunage*.

An *ajiro gaki* (plaited bamboo fence) is a bit labor intensive to build, but the result is both beautiful and strong.

The *nure-en* here is rather narrow but provides an important interface between house and garden. I show how to build an *ajiro gaki* and *nure-en* following the next section.

TOP TO BOTTOM: *Oribe* lantern and footing stone water basin. *Daisugi* and full moon maple help conceal the background. The open weave side of the *ajiro gaki* faces the lawn. The *nure-en* provides a place to relax outdoors.

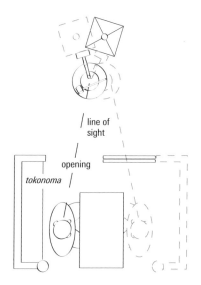

Work begins on planting even as the fence is going up.

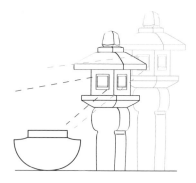

Setting the basin and lantern relative to the main viewing position.

line of sight

opening

tokonoma

Greater height of lantern=greater distance from basin.

CREATING THE GARDEN

The first thing to decide is the finished ground level of the garden and the transition in height from the floor level of the architecture to the shoe-removing stone (*kutsunugi-ishi*) to the stepping stones, and finally to the moss and sand. Flatten the ground level with the help of a level gauge and leveling string.

Next, the total space is marked on the ground with lime, and the bamboo fence is constructed and set in place, leaving one side open until all the materials are brought into the space. After that, the *nure-en* is built. Now, the position and height of the stone lantern and stone basin are decided. To do this, have someone hold the lantern while you sit in the proper viewing position inside the house (illustration left). The lantern should be to the right if the seating position is on the left and reversed if the seating position is on the right. The stone basin is placed in front of the lantern, a little closer to the center of the primary view. The front of the lantern's light box should face the center of the water basin. The height of the water basin is adjusted so that the water can be seen clearly and the view is not interrupted by the *nure-en*. Stand the basin on blocks of wood until the dirt is mounded or base stone set to support it. Keep in mind that the doors in the photo (bottom right) have been removed to show the garden more completely. Normally, one half is blocked by the sliding glass door and paper screen (*shoji*). The height of the lantern should be adjusted in relation to the height of the *chozubachi*. Light from the lantern is supposed to illuminate the area where hands are washed. Generally speaking, the taller the lantern, the further back it should be from the *chozubachi*.

The cedar has been trained in the vertical-branch *daisugi* style and is placed next in the best position to block the view of the electric pole. This evergreen will grow straight and tall but not wide. One point to note here is that although the processes in this book are listed in order for the sake of instruction, at every step of making a garden you need to be conscious of the previous and following steps at the same time. In the case of planting the cedar, for example, I am conscious of how much space it will require between the lantern and the fence, even as I am concentrating on the position of the lantern in relation to the view from the room. Keep in mind that every element is subject to change and adjustment as you go along. In fact, working on a small *tsubo niwa*—like some of those featured in this chapter—is good practice before attempting a larger work.

Next, the *momiji* is planted. This tree is rather slender at the base but has an interesting shape due to the multiple trunks. The canopy will grow to no more than 2 to 3½ yards (2 to 3 m) across as the tree matures to its full height. After that, *kakuremino* is planted before the stepping stones are placed along with the shoe-removal stone. Then the soil is mounded around the lantern, basin, and trees (following the lines marked in lime), then dug out where the decorative stones are set. Considering the size of the garden and the need to place the stones away from the fence, the stones should be small. In this setting, they play a supporting role to the lantern and basin and are set so they "look back" toward the lantern to form a triangular grouping with it.

A drain is dug and a PVC pipe inserted with the mouth of the drain just to the front of the basin (hidden by the flat round stones in the photo). At the same time, the position of the *kakehi* is decided and a trench for the incoming water is dug (I discussed making a simple *kakehi* on pages 44 and 45.). In positioning the *kakehi*, keep several points in mind. The water that arches out of the bamboo spout should fall roughly one third into the *chozubachi*, so as not to hit the ladle (*hishaku*) laid across it. The height of the spout should be enough to let you scoop water from between the spout and the basin comfortably (about 4 to 6 inches/10 to 15 cm). The *kakehi* should not line up directly between the basin and the lantern. If the lantern is on the right, the *kakehi* should be somewhere to the left of it.

Some additional plantings are added to give variety of form and color close to the ground level. In this case I chose a dwarf rhododendron with a pink flower. Finally, moss is planted all over the mounded soil and sand is spread over the remaining areas of the garden. In this case, no pattern will be raked, so a depth of 1 to 1 ½ inches (2 to 3 cm) of ⅛-inch (3-mm) diameter sand is enough. In deciding the balance between moss and sand, remember that the larger the moss-covered area, the more calming the garden, but at the same time the garden will lose its crispness. The larger the sand-covered area, the greater the tension, but the sand must be laid level and kept clean.

The mounded earth and moss unify the various elements into a single group.

For those seated in the room, this small garden expands the space in a warm and comforting way.

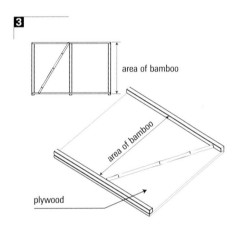

2

78.8"   78.8"

1²⁄₃ x 4³⁄₄" hanbashira

side view

1¼ x 1²⁄₃"

1²⁄₃ x 4³⁄₄"
1¼ x 1²⁄₃"
1²⁄₃ x 4³⁄₄"

3

area of bamboo

area of bamboo

plywood

5

center

5 "white" strips

5 "green" strips

CREATING AN *AJIRO GAKI* PLAITED BAMBOO FENCE

To turn this space into a garden, it was imperative to enclose it in some fashion. For this purpose we constructed a tall, 2-yard (1.8-m) bamboo fence. The street and neighbor's sides were completely shut out, but the third side (facing the other half of the owner's property) was made with an open weave. This created both interesting light patterns and a way for a light breeze to penetrate the garden on a hot afternoon. In addition, we added a narrow *nure-en* to this featureless building to improve the connection with the garden and make life a little more comfortable.

1. After moving the storage away from the house, we decided the *warima* (best-looking proportion) for the fence. The height needed to be kept tall to minimize the view of the surroundings and we needed to keep to the width of the room and to a depth that allowed access to the metal storage shed behind. This dictated a shape that was almost square, which is less than ideal for a Japanese garden. Using the open-weave on one side helped to break up this symmetry. The proportions of a fence or wall normally depend partly on the view from inside the house, partly on the surroundings, and partly on the physical space inside the garden.

2. We used 1²⁄₃ x 4³⁄₄-inch (4 x 12-cm) vertical posts called *hanbashira*— which means "half-post" in Japanese because they are half the size of a post used in building a traditional-style home. Three posts are inserted in the ground. The center post is a little shorter than the outer posts. 1¼ x 1²⁄₃-inch (3 x 4-cm) strips are nailed between the posts at the base. At the top, nail strips to the inside of the outer posts, and above the center post. Finally, nail another *hanbashira* above the top strip.

3. With the frame basically complete, we begin construction of the weave by placing a sheet of plywood—a little larger than the height of the fence—on the ground, to use as a work surface. Nail strips of wood along the bottom and top so that the inside dimension between them is equal to the outside dimension of the 1¼-inch horizontal strips.

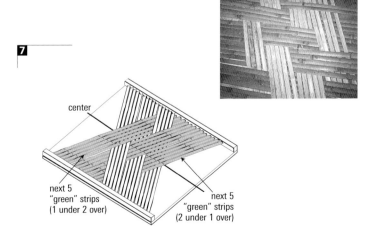

6

center

1 set over
2 sets under

next 5 "white" strips

7

center

next 5 "green" strips (1 under 2 over)

next 5 "green" strips (2 under 1 over)

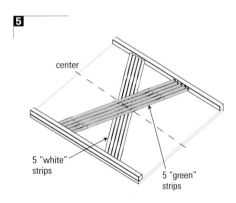

4. The soft bamboo we use for this weave is especially thin and prepared for this purpose by having the interior nodes scraped off. Such material is increasingly difficult to obtain even in Japan. If you find the material, this is still a difficult fence to make even for an experienced gardener. I recommend building a small fence first—perhaps a sleeve fence (*sode gaki*)—for practice. Before beginning, sort your strips of bamboo to eliminate any pieces that curve or are too short. Save the short pieces for the end and use the curved strips for something else.

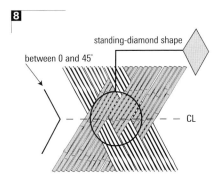

5. Take five strips and lay them side by side at an angle, with the back (white side) of the bamboo up, and the top and bottom edges resting against the wood strips you previously nailed to the plywood. Take the next five strips and lay them across the first in the opposite direction, this time with the front (green side) of the bamboo up. The crossing point should be roughly at the center of the plywood board.

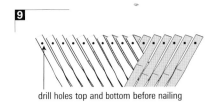

drill holes top and bottom before nailing

6. Lay five more white strips on both sides of the first five white strips, but slide one side under the first green strips you laid down, and one side on top. The weave we are making will have a two over, two under pattern.

7. Slide five more green strips next to the first five, in such a way that they lie under one set of white strips, and above the next two white sets. Take two more sets of five green strips and slide them in on both sides of the first five. This time the pattern should be reversed—two over and one under. This is the first complete weave and the strips begin to lock in place.

8. Work slowly and continue to add strips using a wooden mallet, tapping in the strips so that no gaps appear. Remember to keep alternating front to back so your fence will have the same appearance on both sides. For this fence keep the angle of the weave between 0 and 45 degrees. The appearance should be like standing diamonds, not squares or horizontal diamonds.

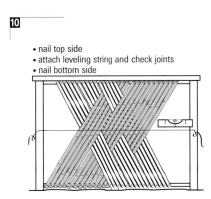

9. Before the weave gets too heavy we will stand it up and begin nailing it to the frame. This will require two or three people. Drill holes in the top edges of the strips for nails and stand the weave. Nail the top edges along the upper horizontal wooden strips so that they are tight against each other. Make sure your bamboo goes from the top to the bottom horizontal wooden strips.

10. Run a level, horizontal string across the whole fence. Check that the points where the bamboo crosses are level. They will have a tendency to shift as you progress. Constant checking ensures a consistent angle of the weave from beginning to end. Start nailing in the bottom of the bamboo while checking, adjusting, and tightening the weave.

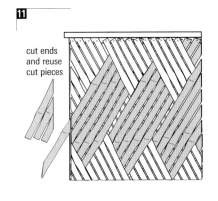

11. Now, in the standing position, keep adding strips to the weave as before. As you get closer to one of the vertical posts, you will need to cut the bamboo shorter. Keep drilling and nailing the top and bottom of the strips until you complete the span. Use flooring nails to secure the bamboo and be careful—bamboo splits easily.

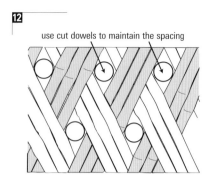

12

use cut dowels to maintain the spacing

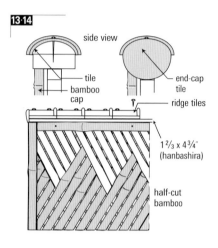

13·14

side view

tile
bamboo
cap

end-cap
tile

ridge tiles

1²⁄₃ x 4³⁄₄"
(hanbashira)

half-cut
bamboo

12. For the open weave side of the fence, use three strips instead of five, and create a space between each succeeding group of about two strips wide. Keep this space even by sticking a wood dowel of just the right diameter between the rows until you have them nailed down. Remove the dowels and use them for the next row. The open weave will be a simple one up, one down pattern, unlike the two up, two down of the rest of the fence.

13. When finished with the weaving, split long lengths of bamboo—with a 1²⁄₃ to 2-inch (4 to 5-cm) diameter—in half, and use them to cover the ends of the weave on top, bottom, and both sides.

The back side exposes the frame but the weave is identical to the front side.

The completed garden, *nure-en*, and fence.

14. We use ridge roofing tiles to cover the top of the fence. These are secured with nails but be careful not to nail down too hard and break the ceramic tile.

15. To preserve the fence, I coat it with a fungicide, a mold-killing kitchen or bathroom cleaner mixed with water, or just bleach. I brush this liberally onto the bamboo and let it soak in. Mold growth, not dirt, is the chief cause of bamboo turning dark with age. Wait several weeks before coating the fence.

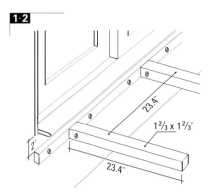

CREATING A *NURE-EN* DECK

As the fence is being finished we start constructing the *nure-en*. This one is rather narrow at 24 inches (60 cm) but good enough to accommodate one *zabuton* (Japanese-style cushion). If you have the space, 35½ inches (90 cm) is ideal. For the *nure-en* we used Douglas fir (*bei matsu*).

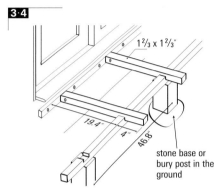

1. We build the base by first running a 1¼ x 1⅔-inch (3 x 4-cm) strip along the wall of the house, a bit more than 2 inches (5 cm) under the lip of the aluminum frame sliding doors. Depending on your building's material, use the appropriate anchor bolts to hold this in place.

2. To this we attach, at a 90-degree angle, 1⅔ x 1⅔-inch (4 x 4-cm) pieces of wood, about 24 inches (60 cm) in length, at a pitch of 24 inches (60 cm) center to center. Screw these in at an angle through the side.

3. Next comes the 1⅔ x 1⅔-inch (4 x 4-cm) front support that is notched to hold the pieces of wood coming out from the wall. This is set about 20 inches (50 cm) from the wall-side support so that the pieces resting on it extend beyond it by about 4 inches (10 cm).

4. To support this, we use wood blocks of about 4 x 4 inches (10 x 10 cm). They can be inserted in the ground or placed on support stones as you like, and this will determine their length. The pitch between the legs is 47 inches (120 cm).

5. For the surface of the *nure-en* we use 1¼ x 2-inch (3 x 5-cm) runners of 3.2 to 4.3 yards (3 to 4 m) in length, standing on their sides with a gap between them of ¼ to ⅖ inch (6 to 10 mm). You will need to screw these in from underneath, so leave yourself enough room to get in with an electric driver. The gap between the runners should be enough to let rain through but not enough to see clearly through the *nure-en*. Even so, the wood will rot in time, usually at the point furthest from the house. This is one good reason to use the runners parallel to the house rather than perpendicular. When the outer runners show signs of rot, they can be replaced easily. I usually use a slightly wider runner for the edge of the *nure-en*.

6. Complete the *nure-en* with a coat of oil stain in a mid-brown color. The frame and runners should be coated before final assembly. To step from the *nure-en* to the ground level, we use a large, squared-off *kutsunugi-ishi* of one half to three quarters the height of the *nure-en*.

The completed frame.

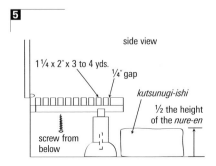

The completed *tsukubai*.

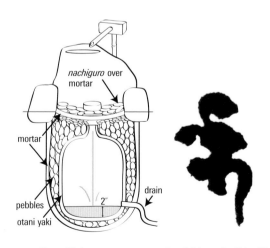

Overall view of the *kare sansui* garden.

The *suikinkutsu* arrangement under the *tsukubai*.

Sanskrit letter for *Yakushi*.

nachiguro over mortar

mortar

pebbles

otani yaki

drain

2"

- ### Creating a *Tsukubai* Arrangement with a *Suikinkutsu* (Water *Koto* Chamber)

This dry landscape (*kare sansui*) courtyard garden was made for a doctor. Accordingly, I choose the symbolic theme of the "healing Buddha" (*Yakushi*) and arranged mounded earth and moss in the shape of the Sanskrit character representing the *Yakushi* Buddha. I created a Buddhist triad stone arrangement (*sanzon-seki*), comprising a slender central stone (*chuson-seki*) and larger side stones (*kyoji-seki*), made with mountain stones brought from northern Japan. At the center of the garden, a stone lantern and a crouching basin (*tsukubai*) arrangement were laid out to face the Japanese-style drawing room (*shoin*).

A typical *tsukubai* arrangement is composed of the rear stone (*kagami-ishi*), basin (*chozubachi*), waterspout (*kakehi*), hot water vessel stone (*yuto-ishi*), the candlestick stone (*teshoku-ishi*), and the front stone where the person using the basin stands. The *yuto-ishi* and *teshoku-ishi* are often more symbolic than practical. A drain is also created in front of the basin and covered with rounded pebbles. In this case, a *suikinkutsu* has also been installed under the drain. This is a device for creating a pleasant sound from the draining water.

For the *suikinkutsu*, I often use a vessel of *otani yaki*, a type of ceramic from Tokushima, specially made for this purpose. I first dig out a hole a little larger and deeper than the ceramic vessel and mortar the sides of the hole. It is also possible to use a section of cement pipe for this. Once dry, I place some large rounded stones (*goro-ishi*) at the bottom and place the vessel on top of them. After connecting the drainpipe to the hole in the side of the *otani yaki*, I fill the space around and above the vessel with the same stones. A mesh is placed over the inlet of the vessel and smaller stones are packed in across the entire top. Again, mortar is used to make a curved basin for the *tsukubai*, leaving a hole in the middle for water to drain through. Black *nachiguro* stones are used to fill the basin and the drain is topped with a piece of roofing tile. Finally, a few plants are added to taste. In this case, I planted a rare wild flower from Shikoku—a perennial— along with some ferns.

When the sound from the *suikinkutsu* is properly adjusted, it is rather high pitched, almost like a wind chime made of slate, rather than the drip, drop sound of falling water.

- ### *Yukimi-mado* and *Mitatemono* in a Small *Tsubo Niwa*

In the case of this residence, because the surrounding wall is low, the neighbors' houses, telephone poles, and street signs jump into view when looking out on the garden. The *yukimi-mado* (snow-viewing window) is an ingenious way of hiding eyesores outside the house while focusing the view on the garden.

Two key points about Japanese gardens is that they are viewed

Yukimi-mado with the bottom half raised to view the garden.

while sitting on the floor inside the house, and this view has developed without incorporating the sky into the picture. Aside from the present-day merits of cutting out unsightly objects outside the garden, Japanese aesthetics have developed along these lines since ancient times. The garden is traditionally located on the south side of the house where the light is strong. *Shoin*-style buildings of the Ancient and Classical eras used *shitomido* that hung on hinges and opened upward. The sitting position was set far back into the room. Coupled with the deep overhang of the roof, the result was a low-slung panoramic view of the garden. With the change to *shoin*-style architecture, the building became smaller and the sitting position became closer to the garden, but the view of the sky was still restricted. With *sukiya*-style architecture, the viewer comes to the edge of the building and the *engawa* and *nure-en* become a place, literally, to sit in the sun. The combination of practical needs and ancient aesthetics results in features such as the *yukimi-mado* that opens vertically to let in filtered light without showing the sky.

The garden itself is minimal, containing only an *Oribe* lantern and some plantings beside a tall water basin surrounded by moss. A low basin could not have been seen from a seated position. This water basin has a long, gear-like shape and was probably once part of a watermill. A small basin has been carved into the top and the original hole that penetrated the entire stone has been sealed. This is a fine *mitatemono*—an old object reused in a new way. The root word *"mitateru"* means to reuse or re-see a thing. The concept seems to have developed with the tea garden. The point of using objects like this lies in entertaining oneself and one's guests by using something cleverly in a way other than for what it was originally intended. In gardens, *mitatemono* are usually stone objects and are used for such purposes as water basins, stepping stones, shoe-removing stones, and lanterns.

Space between house and exterior wall is minimal.

■ Creating a Small Courtyard Garden for Your Living Room

The room pictured here is a large tearoom (*hiroma chashitsu*) inside a residence. This house was newly built, but you can do the same thing to an existing room by punching out the wall and building a small *tsubo niwa* adjacent to it. This window was built low and wide (about 1.3 x 2 yards / 1.2 x 1.8 m) for two reasons: to give an unobstructed view of the garden and to serve as a crawl-through entrance (*nijiriguchi*) for the tea master and her guests. Conventional windows in a Japanese-style room have two to four horizontally sliding glass panels and *shoji* screens, but this window was constructed with a single glass panel and a single *shoji* screen that can be hidden away in the wall. In winter, when the window is closed, the garden view is unobstructed.

In designing the garden, I found inspiration in a woodblock print (*ukiyo-e*) by Katsushika Hokusai. Through his technique of extending objects outside the frame, the viewer is able to envision their entire shape. Similarly, presenting a partial view of the garden from a low angle—behind an architectural frame—I tried to conjure an image of expanse. Seeing mostly the stems of the bamboo planted there, the viewer imagines lush green leaves growing above.

The most conspicuous element in this small garden is the back wall. A stone block wall was built around the property, but I felt it was too rough for this garden. I wanted a softer appearance and therefore used strips of cedar bark. Although it darkens this diminutive garden, it adds a rustic elegance. Achieving elegance is of particular importance in garden making and a key goal in Japanese culture.

The length of the opening affords a full view of the garden when the doors are slid back into the wall cavity. This required special treatment of the building structure. For an existing room, split the door into several pieces to slide right and left into smaller wall cavities. This *tsubo niwa* is exactly one *tsubo* (3.6 square yards / 3.3 sq m). The *tobi-ishi* leading off to the right define this window as an entrance to the tearoom.

1. First, vertical strips of 1.7 x 1.7-inch (4.5 x 4.5-cm) wood are anchored to the block wall and furring strips are screwed in horizontally above that at a pitch of about 20 inches (50 cm) on center.

2. The strips of rough cedar bark, 12 inches (30 cm) wide x 2 yards (1.8 m) tall x ¼ to ⅖ inch (6 to 10 mm) thick, are nailed vertically on top of this. The nailheads are kept in a straight, horizontal line. Narrow, whole bamboo of about ⅗ to ¾ inch (15 to 20 mm) diameter is nailed on top of them to cover them up. Brass nails are used for this.

A *tsubo niwa* creates a restful, contemplative atmosphere, turning a simple room into a teahouse.

3. With the wall finished, golden bamboo (*hotei chiku*) is planted to form a small grove on the left side. *Hotei* bamboo will grow 6½ to 8¾ yards (6 to 8 m) tall in warm climates, but in a cold climate it will stay short and slim. The key point of this bamboo is that the nodes are close together and prominent near ground level, giving the bamboo more form and detail. Another aspect of bamboo, other than the slender elegance of its form, is the way the leaves catch the light and bring it down into the space against the dark cedar background.

4. Most bamboo has two branches extending from each node. To enhance its feeling of delicacy, one of these is often cut off. Which one will depend partly on how best to make the trees complement each other. Twisted branches are also removed and all the branches along the bottom third have been removed to emphasize the fine delicateness of the plant.

5. Bamboo gets old in three to five years and should be cut down. To do this, dig out some dirt around the base and cut it below ground level. Cover with dirt and moss. Bamboo is categorized into "clumping" or "running" types. To keep the running type from spreading outside the desired area, a barrier of concrete, block, sheet metal, etc., needs to surround the area to a depth of at least 24 inches (60 cm). The barrier should come up just past ground level to prevent rhizomes from crawling over the top edge.

6. I next planted moss and dragon's beard grass (*ryu no hige*) on a roughly shaped bed of *yamazuna* to set the atmosphere of a deep, mountain grove.

7. I set *Kurama-ishi* stepping stones across the front of the space, leading from left to right and veering away from the entrance to join the walkway around the side of the house. The *kutsunugi-ishi* is placed to the right to indicate the entrance to the *chashitsu*. The stepping stones are quite small and set low, as befits the size of the garden. The floor of this *chashitsu* is also built quite low to the ground to make it easier for guests in kimono to enter and to give it a more intimate connection with the garden.

8. Next I added two small blue stones (*ao-ishi*) for resting a small bronze lantern on. One stone is higher and closer to the building, one lower and further away. When a ceremony is underway, the lantern is extinguished and placed close to the room. The color of the stone is a good match for the blue-green rust of the bronze, giving stone and lantern the feeling of joining together. Though stones are often placed first and moss planted almost last, the narrow depth of this garden made it better to work from back to front.

9. Finally, *Shirakawa* sand of about ⅖ inch (10 mm) diameter and 1¼ inch (3 cm) depth is placed around the stepping stones to complete the garden.

▶ TOP TO BOTTOM: Exterior wall before and during application of the cedar bark, followed by preparation of the garden and the finished work.

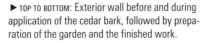

This *machiya tsubo niwa* takes full advantage of a limited space (above) to bring nature into close contact with the living and working environment (below).

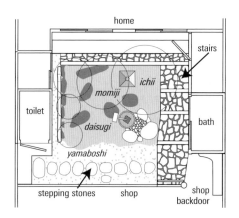

■ *Tsubo Niwa* in a Kyoto-style Townhouse

This courtyard garden is in a kimono shop operating in a Kyoto-style townhouse (*machiya* or *omoteya*). This type of building is long and narrow (about 8.7 yards / 8 m wide by 44 to 55 yards / 40 to 50 m deep), with a shop in the front and a residence in the back. Because of the length of the house and the closeness of neighbors to the right and left, light and fresh air tend to decrease as one goes deeper into the house. To ease this situation, the house is punctuated by open spaces.

This particular house is unusual in that there is a difference in level between the shop in the front and residence in the rear of just over a yard (1 m). Positioned in between, the previous garden contained a small pond and waterfall in this tiny 24 square-yard (22 sq-m) space. It also had rough stones arranged as steps. To begin the new garden, we removed all this in wheelbarrows through the shop, which was also being renovated. We reused many of the existing stones, and two tall trees—a yew (*ichii*) and a maple (*yama momiji*)—were used just as they stood.

As this is a kimono shop, we decided on a tea garden style. First the ground had to be leveled (except for the area around the roots). To the left of the garden is the toilet, which is used by customers and shop staff. 1.6 yards (1.5 m) of space, closest to the shop, will remain flat and be used for stepping stones to walk between the toilet and shop. From that point to the higher level of the residence, dirt is piled up; and the *Oribe*-style lantern is set amidst the trees.

To make it easier for women in kimono to walk between the house and shop, we decided to make a rather broad staircase from rounded river stones and cut-granite edge stones. This surface was carried up to the area in front of the residence as well. The soil under the stairs was pounded down and leveled. The granite and the stones for the side of the stair were set first. Then, the river stones were filled in, one step at a time, in a bed of mortar, and the joints were filled with mortar mixed with black ink, giving it a more formal feeling. The work was difficult since the roots of these large trees were tightly packed in the space. In addition, on the right side of the garden there is a Japanese-style bath (*ofuro*) used by the residents. Access is from the second and third steps of this staircase. I also designed the doors for this bathroom, along with the walls of the garden, the residence entrance, and the rear entrance of the shop.

With the staircase done, the *tsukubai*, stones, and stepping stones were placed next. In addition to the existing trees I added a small *daisugi* and *yamaboshi*. Finally, the sloped area is covered in dragon's beard grass (*ryu no hige*)—which is shade tolerant—to complete the garden.

■ A *Tsubo Niwa* for a Medical Clinic

Dr. Ishikawa was building a new clinic and consulted me about building a garden. He is a doctor of internal medicine, but he planned to combine Western and Eastern medicine, including acupuncture, massage, and counseling. His philosophy is based on healing the mind and body together, and his belief in hands-on experience in everything lead him to fully participate in building the garden. The theme of the garden is "a healing garden of the four seasons."

The property was located next to a noisy two-story garage. To get some peace and quiet, we built a sizable 4.3-yard (4-m) tall concrete wall to block it out. Rather than push the house and clinic up against the wall (and try to ignore it), we located the house away from it and created a courtyard garden space. I designed the wall to be a gentle backdrop for this garden by covering the upper third with horizontal bamboo in a *misu gaki* style, mixing four types and widths of bamboo to add texture. Below that, I created a separation with Japanese roof tiles, in order to give some relief to the wall and reduce the visual scale. Then I sprayed the section below in a tone similar to a clay wall (*dobei*).

With the basic layout set, we discussed with the architect how to create the most relaxing setting for patients. The result was a *sukiya*-style building quite unlike a clinic. Half of the examination rooms are arrayed along the garden side, divided only by large *shoji* screens. The sides of the rooms facing the garden are completely open. This side of the building is floor-to-ceiling glass with a glass door at one end. The result is a panoramic view.

The doctor's private office is a *tatami*-matted room with a tearoom atmosphere. The office and examination rooms form an L shape facing the garden. Around both sides of the L, we built a 35½-inch (90-cm) deep *nure-en*, covered with a deep eave, supported on posts at the outside edge. Views of the garden from these two sides, plus one corner of another examination room, were all equally important. I decided on a round focal point: a large *chozubachi* made from the base of a *gorinto* (five-elements tower). I placed this off-center of the garden toward the private office/tearoom and laid stepping stones from there to the office. Another path of stepping stones leads from the far side of this office, across the garden, and past the second group of examination rooms beyond. Along the way they encounter a staggered *nobedan* made of label stones (*tanzaku-ishi*) and rounded river stones.

The trees are primarily deciduous, tailored to maximize the effects of the seasons on the garden. *Momiji, yamaboshi, hauchiwa kaede*, and camellia (*tsubaki*) are the main trees. I set stones at the bases of these trees to add visual stability (*nejime*). The doctor insisted on covering the entire garden with haircap moss (*sugigoke*), as he felt that the softness of the green moss was very soothing. I therefore planted the trees rather sparsely—as direct sunlight enters the garden for a limited number of hours per day—and I instructed him on gathering moss from an area with similar growing conditions. We combined this with purchased material, and I believe the results of our overall collaboration will give sustenance to him and his patients for years to come.

An atmosphere to ease a patient's mind: a *sukiya*-style clinic and garden.

The view from the doctor's tearoom-like office, showing the length of the garden and the examination rooms on the right.

"ANCIENT" DRY LANDSCAPE GARDEN FOR A MODERN THREE-STORY RESIDENCE

A new three-story reinforced concrete residence was being built to replace Dr. Ishizone's old wooden house, and the gardens were to be remade at the same time. Of the four gardens made for this new house, the two main ones were a long approach garden (see Chapter 1), and a courtyard garden. The request for the courtyard garden was for one that blends with the Western-style building and that can be appreciated not only from the first floor but from the second and third floors as well. I therefore aimed for a garden that is fairly innovative but does not lose sight of the essence of the Japanese garden, which I believe to be *miyabi*—the state of being beautiful, clean, and elegant.

It has been said that *miyabi* was a light-hearted aesthetic of the Classical era, and that it gave way to the more somber aesthetic of *mono no aware*—a melancholy sense of being moved by the ephemeral beauty of things. During the Medieval era, constant war, the spartan simplicity of Zen, and the *wabi* aesthetic, projected an austere and undecorated sense that colored the Japanese arts with a spiritual, serious, and somber mood. Not always as evident is that *miyabi* continued to inform the light-hearted aspect of Japanese humanism, which shows itself in the raucous splendor of *kabuki* performance, the humanity of *yamato-e* painting, the refined art of *maki-e* gilded lacquer, and the lively art of *ukiyo-e*. I always try to embody this sense of "refinement with a light touch" in my work.

THEME, LAYOUT, AND ELEMENTS

The overall theme of this work was "seeing a garden from every room." Accordingly, there are four separate gardens, the main two being the approach and courtyard gardens. These gardens are visually independent and each have their own theme. The approach garden uses a design theme something like "a tree garden to journey through the seasons." A different type of journey takes place in the courtyard garden, which takes a traditional crane (*tsuru*) and turtle (*kame*) island theme. The journey here is across a stone bridge and through an ocean of sand.

The owner is a doctor who runs a clinic located in front of the residence. It was decided that a flat, broad walkway was needed for the approach garden. I set cut granite in a diamond pattern, into a base of *arai dashi. Arai dashi* is concrete mixed with ¾ to 1¼-inch (2 to 3-cm) pebbles. Before the concrete has completely hardened, the surface is scrubbed with a stiff brush and water to expose the aggregate.

The courtyard garden is made to be viewed from three sides and from the first, second, and third floors. For inspiration on how to handle this, I turned to the work of Shigemori Mirei, whose garden for the Kishiwada castle in Wakayama Prefecture makes a strong impression when viewed from the castle above.

There were some very old trees on the site, and I fought both the contractor

LEFT: A stone bridge surmounts a sea of *sabi jari*, as a two-meter stone lantern looks on from an island of moss and ancient trees. RIGHT: Detail of *araidashi* (exposed aggregate) walkway of the approach garden.

and the client to preserve them. Three in particular—a red pine (*aka matsu*) about 7.6 yards (7 m) in height and between 150 and 200 years old, an equally large black pine, and a large yew (*ichii*)—became prominent elements in the new design. After ten years in their new positions, they are thriving, and the beauty of their weathered bark is an irreplaceable part of the history of this garden.

Ao-ishi from the Shikoku region were used prominently in this garden to create the crane-and-turtle image. A *kiyotaki dera*-style lantern, a beautiful reproduction of one found in the Daigoji temple in Kyoto, was chosen to match the ancient trees. A large and forceful lantern was needed to "compete" with the scale of these trees. A coin-shaped (*fusen-gata*) basin was set close to the house to create an accent in the foreground—when viewed from the living room on the first floor. A tall *Katsura gaki* along the open end created by the U-shaped architecture interrupts the view of the old wooden clinic next door. Brown gravel (*sabi jari*) was used to give the entire garden a subdued air and reduce the glare that would be caused by white sand.

The previous garden on this site was a pond garden, and the owner—who grew up with it—and his wife wanted a radical change. I chose to make a *kare sansui* to add a quiet air of contemplation to the busy lives of the doctor and his family. The mounded soil and moss is shaped as a crane and turtle, with the long neck of the crane stretching toward the house. Stones are set to represent the main features of the turtle and the crane.

There are two additional *tsubo niwa* gardens. One, located to the left of the house (looking from the street side), is adjacent to the *butsuma*, a room containing a Buddhist shrine to the ancestors of the family. For this simple garden I placed one lantern in a sea of sand and made a 3.2 to 4.3-yard (3 to 4-m) hedge (*ike gaki*) from *Quercus myrsinaefolia* (*shirakashi*), a broadleaf evergreen of the oak family.

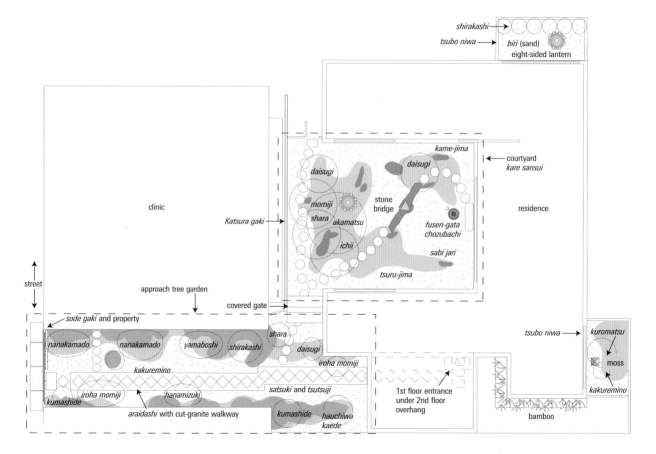

The *tsubo niwa* at the back of the house contains the tall black pine, which had to be planted before the building was even constructed as there was no way of getting it in after. This pine was in rather poor condition and no one believed it could be saved. I cut back the branches severely and, after planting it, had it covered with a black mesh material for about one-and-a-half years to keep off the wind and the direct sun. I had the owner spray it with water morning and night and apply a dilute liquid fertilizer around the base once per week. I also had him spray the tree with a second fertilizer to promote leaf growth. When the net was finally removed, the tree was budding and restored to good health.

Elements

The stone bridge is long and low, composed of two natural *ao-ishi* stones with an "island" between. I explain how to construct this bridge later on in the chapter.

The large eight-sided lantern (*hachikaku*) is a faithful reproduction of a Medieval-era design.

The approach is a tree garden of deciduous and evergreen trees. The *kare sansui* and *tsubo niwa* gardens contain 150- to 200-year-old trees, which preserve the history of this home.

An elegant, classic *Katsura gaki* fence encloses one side of the garden. I show how to make this fence later on in the chapter.

Ao-ishi (blue stone) from the Ehime region of Shikoku, often said to be the most desirable garden stone, is used extensively here.

A "sea" of rust-colored sand (*sabi jari*) adds a clean and quiet feeling that complements the stately old trees.

Hachikaku stone lantern.

Approach garden of deciduous trees.

The garden in winter.

A "sea" of rust-colored sand.

After the old garden was disassembled, and before the new building was even made, we transplanted the old black pine to its new home in the area at the back of the building that would become the *tsubo niwa*. This garden is actually visible to the right, when coming into the main entrance.

When it came to the main garden, the ground was leveled and then the trees needed to be brought in by crane and planted before the building was completed. Working this way obviously requires planning, as work is carried out in stages over a long period of time. In addition to the trees, the stones and lantern are also set with a crane, but this is a much smaller type that we call a "crab" (because of its extendible legs). This crane could get in and out of the garden after the building was built.

When using sand over a large area, as in this garden, two points need to be considered. First—drainage grading aside—the ground under the sand must be made flat and level. The drainage grading will be taken up by variations in the thickness of the sand to produce an all-important, perfectly flat top surface. Second, a barrier should be installed between the soil and the sand. In this garden, a layer of mortar (about $3/4$ inch/2 cm) was applied. These days we have good results with a geo-grid synthetic sheeting. This sheeting restricts weed growth while allowing rainwater to penetrate. Restriction of weed growth is the main reason for the barrier, but it is also important to keep the soil from mixing with and tinting the sand. The drainage system is installed before this under-pavement is completed. The sand is always laid in last, after the moss or any other ground cover is planted.

As I mentioned, the *tsubo niwa* next to the *butsuma* employed a single stone lantern in a field of rough sand (*biri*). Because of its original use in Buddhist temples, and because it is still a feature of temples, the stone lantern carries spiritual overtones for the Japanese people. It gives the garden a sense of reverence which sends a message to the viewer that "here is a place for quiet contemplation." A single lantern in a sea of sand underscores the importance of this message.

As a counterpoint, this same sense of reverence is transferred, in the second *tsubo niwa*, to the old, black pine. In contrast to Buddhism, the native Japanese religion, Shinto, considers natural objects like trees or stones as embodiments of god (*kami*). This pine is not shaped in the typical S configuration but stands in its natural state, on a small island of moss, accompanied by a single *kakuremino*.

The approach garden, which is constructed last, is a tree garden tailored for viewing while walking through it. I talk more about Japanese methods of grouping trees in Chapter 3. However, the situation in a long

The garden is tailored for viewing from above as well as ground level.

Finished *Katsura gaki* looking toward the garden entrance and covered gate.

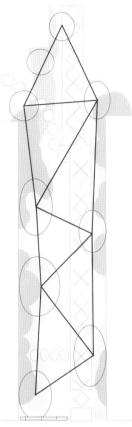

LEFT TO RIGHT: Leveling the ground and planting large trees. Moving and setting stone with crab and *sanmatta*.

The final layout.

Moss and sand laid in and the fence finished.

triangular layout of trees on a long walkway

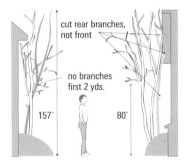

cut rear branches, not front

no branches first 2 yds.

157″   80″

and narrow space through which a person is walking is quite different from the typical garden—which is viewed like a stage setting from a more or less static viewing point. The principles are the same—triangulation, attention to grouping of sizes and types, attention to visual interest throughout the year, and naturalism—but the application is modified by the specific conditions of the space.

This approach is about 5.5 yards (5 m) wide by 33 yards (30 m) long. The area for placing trees is therefore shallow and restricted to a narrow band along both sides of the walkway. In addition to their usual characteristics, trees should be selected on the basis of few branches at lower levels, which could interfere with walking. If these lower branches were simply cut off, it would produce an unsightly appearance closest to the viewer. Tree grouping will also be based on views from opposite ends of the space and the differences in light levels between one side of the path and the other. As the majority of trees are deciduous, we increased the amount of winter greenery by using shaped evergreen azaleas, of no more than 31 ½ inches (80 cm) in height, on both sides of the walkway.

Care needs to be exercised with tall trees in spaces where root growth is restricted on one side, as in this case. Trees should be anchored to each other, with bamboo poles for instance, or to walls using wire at upper levels where it will not be visible. Branches facing the walls will need to be cut whenever their growth threatens to push on the tree and bend it away from the wall.

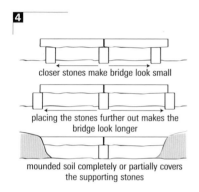

mounded soil height (approx. 12")
bridge thickness (approx. 6")
bridge height (approx. 4")

raked sand level (+1¼ to 1")
ground level (+/−0)

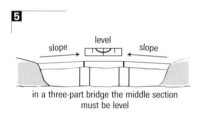

closer stones make bridge look small

placing the stones further out makes the bridge look longer

mounded soil completely or partially covers the supporting stones

slope — level — slope

in a three-part bridge the middle section must be level

■ CREATING A STONE BRIDGE

1. First decide the ground level of the finished sand. This sand will have a raked pattern, so a depth of 1¼ to 2 inches (3 to 5 cm) will be needed. This is a flat garden (*hira niwa*), and the mounded soil for the turtle (*kame-jima*) and crane (*tsuru-jima*) islands on either side of the bridge will be at most 12 inches (30 cm) above ground level. The bridge height should be fixed so that it sits about 4 inches (10 cm) above the *raked* sand and the top surface just meets the finished surface of moss at each end or is slightly below it.

2. The stone for the bridge is naturally flat on one side. Each stone is approximately 1.6 yards (1.5 m) long x 15.7 inches (40 cm) wide x 6 inches (15 cm) thick. In order to maximize the length of the bridge, the stones are placed tip to tip. This left a gap in the center that I later filled with earth and moss, creating a small center island.

3. After the earth on either side is mounded, decide the best angle and position to set the bridge. The stones are placed on wooden blocks until the level and position are adjusted.

4. Once the height and position are decided, one stone at a time is moved aside and the ground at the island side is dug out for the supporting stone (*sukai-ishi*). This stone should be positioned so that less than half is supporting the bridge. If the stone is placed too far under the bridge it will visually shorten the length of the bridge.

5. Even though the height of the island on each side may be slightly different, the bridge should be level. In order to have the bridge *look* level, it is sometimes necessary to raise the center a fraction of an inch (several millimeters) higher than the edges. When bridges are composed of three stones, the outer two stones may be angled slightly up from the edge to the center stone. In that case, the center stone must be absolutely level. Not only level, but in any case where the bridge is composed of two or more slabs, the top of the slabs must also be at exactly the same height. Bridges made of two slabs often use one large stone in the center to support them both. The difference in thickness of the slabs makes this type of assembly difficult to balance.

The bridge stones being set. Notice the small stone on the backside of the center island.

Bridge stones completely set and ground under sand being prepared.

6. Next, in order to stop lateral movement of the bridge, bridge-gripping stones (*hashibasami-ishi*) are placed at the ends and in the middle. These stones should be buried far enough so that they will not move. Sometimes an L-shaped stone is used and lightly tucked under one corner to add to the sense of stability. It is best not to use mortar when setting your stones, as this will make it more difficult to repair in the future.

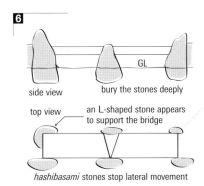

7. The height of these stones should vary and they should never be placed symmetrically. From the example in the photograph, it appears that there is only one *hashibasami-ishi* in the center, but in fact there is a small one on the other side. At least one of the stones at one end of the bridge should stand taller than all the others. This is one type of traditional arrangement.

8. Soil is piled between the two bridge stones and the *hashibasami-ishi* in the middle to fill the gap and create a small center island. Arranging these stones so that they touch only at the longest point has helped extend the length of the bridge, but I did not sacrifice stability. Stability is the main characteristic of a bridge, even a decorative one, and the *hashibasami-ishi* are meant to emphasize that stability and to guide people to walk between them.

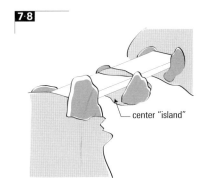

9. Moss is planted on the areas of mounded soil and sand is laid on all the flat areas and raked around the contours of the islands.

After the sand is laid in and raked, notice the difference in the bridge height compared to the photo at the top of the page.

A completed fence.

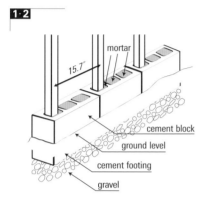

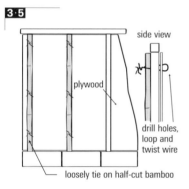

Frame with plywood backing.

To enclose the open side of this garden, we made a tall *Katsura gaki* fence. The fence is named after the original in the garden of Katsura Rikyu. The fence we made here was modified in that the backside was covered in plywood. The traditional fence is visible from both sides and is somewhat more difficult to make. If you want a different finish on the backside, you can cover the plywood surface with quarter-strips of bamboo or vertical wooden planks.

1. Start this fence by laying a row of concrete blocks, secured with mortar, over a foundation of gravel and cement.

2. Stand 1¼ x 1⅔-inch (3 x 4-cm) posts in the holes of the cement blocks at a pitch of approximately 15.7 inches (40 cm). Use the same size wood strips across the top, screwed into the posts, to complete the frame. Check the pitch and temporarily support the fence while checking the verticality with a plumb line. Fill the holes in the cement block with mortar, including those containing the posts, and wait until it sets before starting the next step.

3. Screw ¼ to ¾-inch (6 to 12-mm) waterproof plywood boards to the back of the frame. The boards and frame are then coated with an exterior stain. In our case, the property on the other side of the fence belongs to the same owner. If a fence you are constructing is facing your neighbor's property, it would be a good idea to consult them on the size and material, as they will be living with it at least as much as you!

4. For this fence we use just the branches (*ho*) of *Phyllostachys pubescens* (*moso chiku*) bamboo. Each branch is at least 1.3 to 1.6 yards (1.2 to 1.5 m) in length, and the leaves have been removed but the branchlets are attached.

5. First we take three half-cut bamboo poles of 1⅔ to 2 inch (4 to 5 cm) diameter and loosely secure them over consecutive wooden posts with copper wire. You will need to drill holes through the plywood to pass the wire through, and securing this wire requires two people. The branches will be inserted horizontally between the bamboo and the wooden posts.

6. Branches will need to be sorted before you start. Bamboo branches are curved at the wide end where they grew out of the main shaft. The branchlets grow alternately out of the sides of the branch, with the branchlet closest to the curved end sometimes growing out of the right side, sometimes the left. You want to keep the branchlets, nodes, and curve direction consistent for each row. Separate those with right-starting (*migi-ho*) branchlets from those with left-starting (*hidari-ho*) branchlets.

7. Start with branches with right-starting branchlets and insert the first branch from the top, sliding it in from left to right under all three bamboo poles. The curved end should face outward and "catch" under the vertical half-cut bamboo. Bend down the upper branchlets and tuck them behind the main branch so that all the branchlets are facing down.

8. Insert the next branch and line it up so that the first node is directly in line with the node above. Also make sure that this second branch lies above all

the branchlets from the upper horizontal branch and, likewise, tuck all the new branchlets underneath this second horizontal branch as well.

9. Keep inserting right-starting branches and tucking the branchlets underneath, until a complete row is finished from top to bottom. When you reach the bottom, turn the branchlets up and twist them behind the bottom branches as cleanly as possible. If you find yourself with too many branchlets you can cut some off.

10. By now, you will need to stand and secure two more vertical bamboo halves in order to continue inserting branches. Next, use left-curving branches and insert them from the top, stopping at the third vertical bamboo pole. This adds to the volume of branches just where they are thinning out, allowing a consistent appearance across the length of the fence. Follow the same method as before, keeping the branches tucked together as tightly as possible, until the second row is finished.

11. In this way, the fence will proceed from left to right toward completion. Keep alternating right-curving and left-curving rows and standing vertical bamboo posts as you complete the fence. You will also need to constantly adjust the wire holding the vertical bamboo in place as the gap between it and the wooden post underneath becomes too tight or too loose.

12. As you reach the right side of the fence, the branches will need to be cut shorter until the final ones are the length of exactly two spans of vertical bamboo (approx. 31 inches/80 cm).

13. Complete the fence by taking half-split bamboo of about 3 to 4 inches (7 to 10 cm) diameter and tying one piece over each vertical bamboo pole with *shuronawa*. The tying can be done at an even pitch or randomly, as befits your taste. Likewise, the tops of the vertical bamboo can be cut steeply, as we have done here, or at any angle you like. Finally, use the same half-cut bamboo along the bottom to cover the ends of the posts and along the top to cover the wood frame.

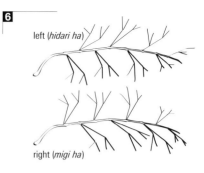

6

left (*hidari ha*)

right (*migi ha*)

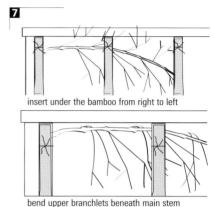

7

insert under the bamboo from right to left

bend upper branchlets beneath main stem

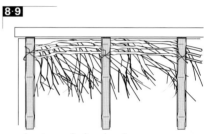

8·9

- insert succesive branches above upper branchlets
- keep bending branchlets behind the main stem and turning down

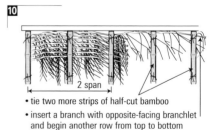

10

2 span

- tie two more strips of half-cut bamboo
- insert a branch with opposite-facing branchlet and begin another row from top to bottom
- add one row of branches for every two spans

13

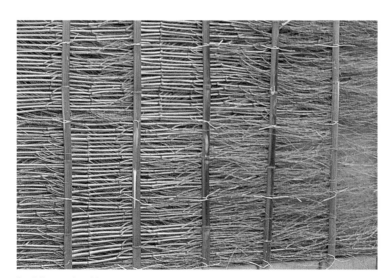

Partially completed fence.

cover horizontal and vertical posts to finish

CLOCKWISE FROM TOP LEFT: *Shirakawa* sand in fine to coarse grades.

RIGHT TO LEFT, TOP TO BOTTOM: *Sabi jari*, *Ise jari*, *Shirakawa* sand, *biri*, white pebble, black *Kobu* pebble.

Sharp-edged gravel holds the shape of the raked pattern.

GARDEN SAND AND PATTERN MAKING

There are many reasons why sand came to be used extensively in Japanese gardens. Some attribute it to influence from the area in front of *shinden* buildings that was covered with sand to provide a place for ritual ceremonies. Others cite the Shinto ritual of purifying sacred areas with white sand. Still others attribute it to the practice in Buddhist temples where sand was used as a manifestation of a state of mind sometimes called "nothingness" (*mu*). With gardens of Kyoto and in the provinces, it is preferable that the ground surface is not laid bare. The soil is full of bacteria, which decomposes things like dead leaves, straw, and animal feces, and when it rains, everything turns to mud. The heat and high humidity of the Kyoto basin add to the fetid, greenhouse atmosphere. People living in bacteria-rich environments are prone to disease, particularly to skin ailments. Covering the soil with clean, dry sand is one way to prevent problems while adding a crisp beauty to the garden.

Several types of sand are commonly used in Japanese gardens (see chart). Every type of sand is sold by grain size in 33 to 44-pound (15 to 20-kilo) bags, or in 1-ton semi-bulk sacks. I choose sands of different grain sizes according to the area to be covered. If the garden is between 3.2 square yards and 22 square yards (3 sq m and 20 sq m), I use *kosu*, or fine sand that has been sieved through a ⅛-inch (3-mm) screen. If the garden is larger than 109 square yards (100 sq m), I use grains of between ⅛ and ⅕ inch (3 and 5 mm), known as *mame*. For the tops of dry waterfalls, I select coarse sand from ⅕ to ⅖ inch (5 to 10 mm) so that the sand does not slip down the edge, and because it suits the image of rough water.

The depth of the sand depends on whether a pattern will be raked or

Shirakawa sand	This is the standard granite sand used in Japanese gardens. This granite river sand originally came from the Shirakawa river in Kyoto, but these days most of this sand comes from mountains in other parts of the country. The sand is light gray but usually considered white.
Sabi jari	This is a granite sand with a high iron content that gives it a rusty color. This sand will get progressively darker as time goes on.
Sakuragawa sand	This is a *sabi jari* from Ibaraki, north of Tokyo. It is distinctive in that its granules are rounded rather than sharp edged.
Oomimaiko sand	A mountain sand from Shiga prefecture that is a cross between *sabi jari* and *Shirakawa* sand.
Ise jari	A sand from Mie prefecture, slightly darker than Oomimaiko.
Biri	*Biri* is a type of mixed sand of natural and crushed material between ⅛ and ⅕ inch (3 and 5 mm) available throughout Japan. It is usually gray, but other colors found in local areas include green, black, and pale pink. This material is cheap and was previously used only in construction.

not. If a pattern were to be raked, a depth of 1 ¼ to 2 inches (3 to 5 cm) would be needed as well as a coarser sand. If not, ¾ to 1 ¼ inches (2 to 3 cm) and a grain size of 1/12 to 1/8 inch (2 to 3 mm) is fine. Under no circumstances use a sand of 1/24 inch (1 mm) or finer, as this will disperse in the wind or compact down when walked on.

It seems that since the fourteenth to fifteenth centuries, patterns—called *samon*—came to be raked into the sand with the intention of representing waves (although other patterns—for instance checkerboard—are sometimes made). The finer the sand, the more attractive the sand patterns, but the more easily the patterns are spoiled by rain. Coarse sand, on the other hand, makes the garden appear rough but holds a pattern well. The color of the sand is chosen according to the garden's theme and location. For example, white sand is good where sunlight is poor, as it reflects light into the house and under trees. This is especially true in traditional Japanese structures, which can be quite dark because the eaves are very deep to prevent rain from entering the house or making the immediate area around the house muddy. On the other hand, in areas with strong light, the glare from white sand can be unbearable. In that case, dark gray or rust-colored sand is a better choice.

Making a simple notched rake.

■ Tools for Sand Patterning

There are no set rules regarding the tools for making patterns in the sand. Often, a simple straw broom is used, especially when fine sand is used or where a strong pattern is not desired. It is sometimes said that the slight lines left in the sand from the rough broom used to sweep it were the original inspiration for creating patterns. To make patterns you may use a bamboo or steel rake like those used for removing leaves or a long block with a row of square or round pegs inserted, or a notched board with a handle attached. I make notched boards from a piece of 0.4 to 0.6 inch (12 to 16 mm) plywood, 8 inches x 12 or 16 inches (20 cm x 30 or 40 cm) depending on the number of notches. These notches are about 4 inches (10 cm) deep. A hole is made in the upper middle of the notched board to accommodate a bamboo or wooden pole. This size rake is used for three or four notches, and such a rake is sufficient for small gardens or where raking is only done around borders and objects. Longer boards with more notches are used for large areas of sand that are raked over their entire surface. Larger rakes require additional strengthening and will be more difficult to pull through the sand. If sand is raked every day, the granules stay loose and easier to reshape. Daily raking also keeps weeds at bay. If you only rake once a week or several times a month, the sand becomes set and more difficult to move. In that case, a metal rake may help to break up the old pattern before laying in the new. In either case, you need to redistribute the sand and make it flat before raking it. For this we use the opposite side of the rake or sometimes an *okame* or a *joren* (borrowed from farming tools). In addition to a rake, a *kogai ita* (also called *tei ita*) is essential equipment for working the sand. This is simply a small piece of wood board with one end cut at an angle. It is used to smooth sand in hard-to-reach places.

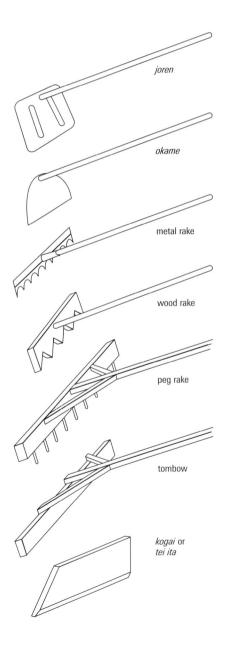

joren

okame

metal rake

wood rake

peg rake

tombow

kogai or *tei ita*

Tea Gardens, Tree Gardens

Around the middle of the Medieval era *cha-no-yu* (tea ceremony) developed, which in turn gave birth to teahouses (*chashitsu*) and to tea gardens, called *cha niwa* or *roji*. Over time *cha-no-yu* became an important influence on dozens of arts and crafts, including architecture, garden making, incense, ceramics, metalworking, flower arrangement, and even matters of etiquette and decorum. As with Buddhism, when it was first introduced to Japan, it spawned whole industries in its service, and became a cornerstone of Japanese culture. I have gradually come to understand this more deeply through my engagement in gardening.

While tea gardens have a long history, tree or "copse" gardens (*zoki-bayashi*) have a history of little over a hundred years and can be considered the newest style of Japanese garden. This development was probably due to the influence of Western garden ideas, and the need to broaden the range of deciduous, untrained trees used in the garden. As a gardener from an area of Japan that just borders on the temperate zone where broadleaf evergreens—the backbone of the traditional garden—are able to flourish, I have put much thought and energy into this style. For those of you who may face a similar situation, I hope the examples in this chapter and this book will be helpful.

TEA GARDEN OF THE AUTHOR'S RESIDENCE

After having run a garden supply store for about a decade, I was getting a lot of garden-making work, as well as frequent visits by my friends and teachers. It occurred to me to build a reception room of minimal size, as I did not have a room for receiving guests. The best thing for that, I concluded, was a four-and-a-half-mat (*yojohan*) tearoom, which I could then use for some real practice in the tea ceremony. I built that tearoom inside the store by adding a sunken hearth (*ro*) to the *tatami*-matted room.

Eventually I closed down the garden supply store and decided to convert the area out back to a tea garden. One day, the stonemason Kinzo Nishimura (whose lanterns are featured throughout this book) called me from his home in Kyoto. "I went to a home today to appraise their stone lantern, and they had a teahouse," he said. "It will be torn down next week and burned with the trees in the garden, so why don't you come take a look? If you like, you can disassemble it and take it home with you."

So I hurried off to Kyoto, took apart the four-and-a-half-mat teahouse, which had been built some eighty years previously, and put everything away in my shed at home. Being a substantial teahouse, it was expensive to rebuild. Nevertheless, I employed the services of a Kyoto master carpenter, Kazuyuki Suzuki, and brought in top-level craftsmen from Kyoto for everything except the concrete foundation. The reconstruction expanded to include demolishing the old courtyard garden and a shed, building an annex onto my old shop and residence, and making a tea garden.

My teahouse (right), annex, and tea garden, looking out from my old tearoom.

Extensive use of stone walkways is one mark of the *Izumo* style.

My old tearoom still serves as a *machiai*.

■ THEME, LAYOUT, AND ELEMENTS

The theme of this garden is "a tea garden in the *Izumo* style." In the Izumo region on the Sea of Japan there is a style of garden that Professor Yoshiki Toda and I have named the *Izumo* style. This style developed amidst a strong culture of tea drinking, long periods of cloudy and snowy weather, and a community of agricultural gentry. As a response to these conditions, a unique style that mixes features of the tea garden and *kare sansui* garden developed. White sand covers the bulk of the area, and the garden, which exists alongside farmland, contains features of the tea garden, including a teahouse. High stepping stones and *tanzaku-ishi*, used boldly and playfully, are prominently featured. For me, the *Izumo* style surpasses the Kyoto style of tea gardens in some respects. It has a clean and bright feeling where Kyoto tea gardens are often dark and heavy. This style is an exquisite regional adaptation of Kyoto garden culture and a strong influence on my work.

My garden is bordered by the main residence and shop, which already existed, and an annex composed of a six-*tatami* (approx. 11 square yards / 10 sq m) and eight-*tatami* (approx. 14 square yards / 13 sq m) Japanese-style living room (*zashiki*), kitchen, and bathroom on the first floor, and a study (*shosai*) and storeroom on the second floor. The annex is used as both a guest house and a teahouse. This addition created an L-shaped architecture, and the teahouse was placed in the open area of the L surrounded by the tea garden.

This teahouse is a *koma* (4.5 *tatami* mats) with 2-mat *mizuya* (lit. water room or kitchen) and a 1-mat *tokonoma,* for a total floor space of less than 15.3 square yards (14 sq m). It contains a rather large window, and both a crawl-through opening (*nijiriguchi*) and a sliding door entrance (*kininguchi*, "noblemen's entrance") for walking in upright.

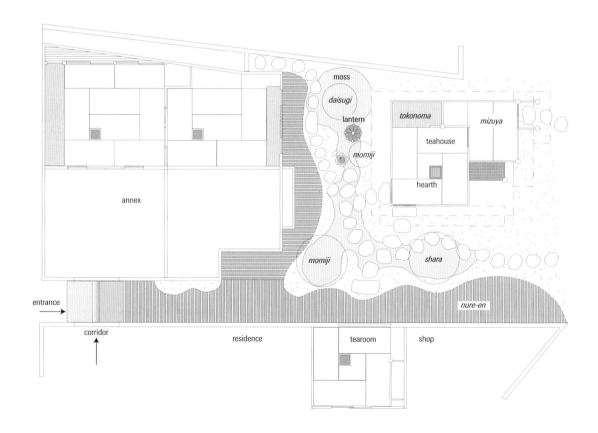

For the tea garden, I dispensed with many of the typical formalities such as a waiting bench (*koshikake machiai*), inner and outer *roji*, fences, gates, etc. This was partly due to the small size of the garden, and partly because I built the annex to serve the function of containing large numbers of guests. For very informal meetings of three or four people, I still use the tearoom inside my former shop.

Facing the room at the back of the annex, I arranged a tall and elegant *chozubachi*, a tall slender lantern that is a reproduction of one from the famous Haeinsa temple in Korea, and planted a *daisugi* to complete the group. This arrangement gives a good view from the tearoom in the shop (shown in the photo on the previous page), a view from the entrance to the shop, and nice views from the rooms in the annex. The teahouse also has a good view of the garden. Though teahouses usually shut out the view of the garden, I am a gardener first and a practitioner of tea second.

The back part of the garden, which is close to the neighbor's house, is enclosed in a tall plaited bamboo fence (*ajiro gaki*). Stepping stones are arranged to lead from the *chozubachi* to the teahouse and Japanese-style room on the far side of the annex. Although I felt the garden too small for the long *tanzaku* stones often used in the *Izumo* style, I did combine sand with the moss, which is an influence from this style.

When everything was finished, I was still unsatisfied with the interplay between the buildings and garden. Though I built a corridor to connect the house and annex, I wanted a shortcut between the shop and annex, plus a way to move outdoors but still feel connected to the house. It may be that the Japanese practice of taking off one's shoes in the house sets up a physiological barrier that distinguishes between going outside and going "out." This results in the desire to have an area outside of the house where one can walk in stocking feet or with slippers. For a Japanese, putting on shoes is the equivalent of leaving. To satisfy these needs, I decided to build a *nure-en* around the inner side of the architecture, which pulled physical and emotional worlds together very nicely.

Elements

This teahouse was salvaged from a Kyoto estate. Most of the woodwork is the original, while the walls, *tatami*, and roofing have been replaced.

A new annex to my house and former shop is an eclectic mix of Western and Japanese-style architecture, typical of the life we lead today.

The *Izumo* style, which has been one of my main influences, uses sand as a ground cover in place of moss or bare soil.

The lantern here is a unique reproduction of a Korean original. Unlike Japanese and most Korean lanterns made of granite, there was a brief period in Korean history when lanterns were made of a blackish stone probably of volcanic origin. This stone proved to be too weak for the purpose and the practice was discontinued. Sculptor Kinzo Nishimura chose black granite from Africa that closely approximates the original but far surpasses it in durability.

With the lantern, I paired a bridge-post (*hashibasami* or *hashigui*) -style *chozubachi* basin with an elegant taper toward the top, crafted by the same sculptor.

The complete teahouse and curving *nure-en*.

TOP TO BOTTOM: The view from the annex. The *Izumo* style. Korean-style lantern and *hashigui* basin.

The original/reproduction of the Haeinsa lantern.

The framework of the teahouse.

CREATING THE GARDEN

For my new courtyard, I sought to make both a tea garden and a garden that is Kyoto style but unlike anything found in Kyoto.

One of my first acts was to commission a replica of a lantern housed in Haeinsa temple in Korea, which is famous as the repository of the *Tripitaka Koreana*—a thirteenth-century Buddhist doctrine carved on more than 81,000 double-sided woodblocks. I often think the stone lantern in the garden is like a necktie on a man: though it is a relatively small part of the overall attire, it stands out above all else. It has a presence stronger than that of garden stones, because it is the most elaborate artificial object in the garden. In my opinion most serious gardeners are diligent students of stone lanterns. It is believed that the lantern was first brought to Japan from Korea in the eighth century. For my own garden I wanted to pay homage to these origins.

I am particularly proud of this lantern, which is the result of my studies in Korea and a book I wrote on Korean-style lanterns and gardens. The original was actually incomplete; only the pedestal, column, shade, and orb existed. Through my studies, I understood what the shape of the original must have been like and commissioned a reproduction based on photos and drawings of the original parts and my design for the light box. Art and craft in Japan and Asia have always been based on copying the masters of past generations until one is able to surpass them. This is both a method of study and a selfless devotion to the craft. Most of these craftsmen are unknown—as is the case with this lantern. But the memory of that effort and devotion to craft remains an inspiration to all of us who continue the tradition.

The main feature of this garden, the teahouse, was constructed before either the garden or the annex. The orientation of the teahouse came first. Though I tried out many configurations on paper, I finally decided to orient the *kininguchi* toward the small tearoom in the shop. This allowed the old tearoom

Finished interior.

to serve as a waiting bench (*machiai*) and was convenient for me to move between the old tearoom and the teahouse—as I do on a regular basis.

For the task of reconstructing the teahouse, I brought in craftsmen from Kyoto. Carpenters that build teahouses are called *sukiya daiku*, and they are among the most highly skilled craftsman in Japan—along with temple-building carpenters known as *miya daiku*. The teahouse was assembled on a concrete and stone footing with the original frame. The walls were reconstructed using a lath made of bamboo and coated with eleven or twelve layers of clay mixed with straw. This is a complicated process involving four or five different clays and eleven or so different types and sizes of straw. The result was very similar to the wall of a teahouse thought to have been made for the famous tea master Sen no Rikyu (1522–91). The doors, windows, and ceiling materials are all the originals, to which a new roof and floor were added.

When it came to the *nure-en*, I was looking for a way to soften the rigidity of the form created by the buildings. Adding a typical *nure-en* would have added to that rigid image, especially considering that it too would need to be an L shape. I finally decided on a wave-like shape, but getting the right curve was difficult. The *nure-en* uses 2-inch (5-cm) square posts standing out perpendicular from the buildings and meeting at a 45-degree angle between the annex and main house. In order to protect it against rain and give it some sense of formality, the wood was painted several times with a dark brown oil-base paint, simulating a lacquer finish. Painting the wood before installation allows for all sides to be coated equally. When dry, the posts were attached in an approximation of the final shape. To make this curve, I experimented using various materials as a guide but finally settled on a typical garden hose filled with water. This could be shaped into a clean S curve, which was then carefully marked on the wood and cut. Finally, the edges were chamfered and painted in red, enhancing the image of a lacquered deck.

Bamboo lath awaits the first coat of clay.

The teahouse in the snow.

Before construction.

■ TEA GARDEN VARIATIONS

■ A Small Front-Yard Tea Garden

This teahouse is attached to the front of the residence of Miss Setsu Takagi. The challenge in this case was to combine approach, front garden, and tea garden all in one, on a small plot of land.

The tea ceremony is a repository of rules and conventions, and virtually every Japanese art has a manual to it. With tea gardens too there are a variety of manuals that are considered standard. Applying that standard to the individual site and to the individual character of the tea master makes each garden unique. The tea master of this house is a woman who teaches tea ceremony for a living. Here I will run through the basic pattern of the tea garden and how we applied it in this case.

The Takagi teahouse is four-and-a-half *tatami* mats plus a one-mat *tokonoma*, built in the *soan* style with only a crawl-through entrance. This pointed toward a diminutive scale and a delicate touch for the garden, as well as an informal feeling befitting a modest house. The entire property was surrounded by a high, rough-cement block wall, totally isolating the garden from the street. It was old and overgrown with vines, adding to a very somber mood. We remade this wall as well as the entire garden, and the total effect from all our changes is a quiet, clean, and light tea garden that makes excellent use of a limited space.

From the entrance of the property to the entrance of the house we created a *so*-style, informal *nobedan* that follows the interior side of the wall around to the entrance of the house. Because there is a drop in elevation from street to entrance of

A modest but complete tea garden for a teacher of tea ceremony.

about 15.7 inches (40 cm), we incorporated two steps into the *nobedan*. This approach garden serves a dual purpose as an outer *roji* (where *nobedan* are often used).

Along the sides of the *nobedan*, we planted moss and black bamboo that is native to this location. We planted the bamboo between the wall and the *nobedan* to lessen the chance that it would spread to other areas. Areas without moss are filled with granite sand, with more sand toward the house.

The *nobedan* turns right at the end to the entrance of the house. Beyond that, several stepping stones and a *kutsunugi-ishi* lead to a room that serves the purpose of a *yoritsuki* (changing or waiting room) for receiving guests before the tea ceremony. Having two entrances so close together, we placed a low *Koetsu sode gaki* to indicate that the actual entrance door was to the right. The *sode gaki* is used in both tea and other types of gardens to interrupt the line of sight, separate space, or show direction.

The approach/outer *roji* is separated from the inner tea garden with a *yotsume gaki* fence commonly used for this purpose. Because this fence is so open and light, it is more an abstract separation than a physical barrier. In Japanese the word *"hei"* means "wall" and indicates a solid barrier. The word *"kaki"* (or *"gaki"* in compounds) means fence. Unlike the Western concept of "fence" (as in "chain-link fence"), the Japanese idea of a fence is something like the "white picket fence"—a visual boundary rather than a strong, physical barrier.

Departing from the *yoritsuki*, where guests leave their belongings, we walk back along the *nobedan* toward the property entrance, this time turning left past it and encountering some stepping stones (*tobi-ishi*) that lead to a waiting bench (*koshikake machiai*), the second stop that the guests at a tea ceremony make. This is usually

New *nobedan* looking from the entrance toward the house.

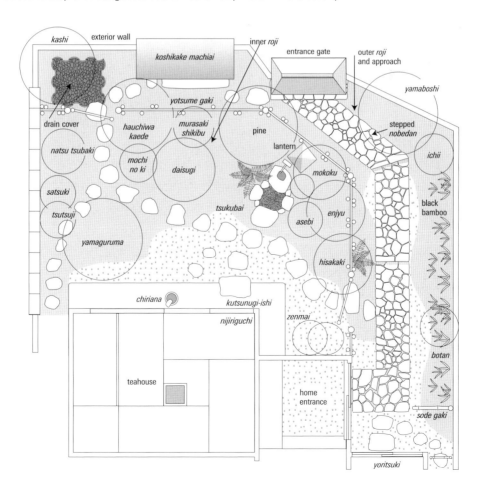

The *nobedan* and outer *roji* looking back from the *yoritsuki*.

The *koshikake machiai* in the outer *roji*.

The *tsukubai* (left) and stepping stones.

composed of a wooden frame, roof, and bench. The bench is 20 to 24 inches (50 to 60 cm) deep and the roof overhangs this by 8 to 12 inches (20 to 30 cm), just enough to keep out a light rain. The frame is usually filled in on three sides with clay, bamboo, or wood. Stones are laid in front of the *koshikake machiai* so that the largest stone is at the side closest to the entrance to the inner *roji*. The other stones may be *tobi-ishi*, *tanzaku-ishi*, or even a small *nobedan*. Once a group of guests is assembled, the tea master will call them to enter the inner *roji* and greet them at the entrance. The entrance to an outer *roji* often contains a roofed gate (in this case the entrance to the property serves that dual role), while the entrance to the inner *roji* is often open, or the gate is an extremely simple, hinged affair called a *shiorido*.

After greeting the guests, the tea master returns to the teahouse while the guests prepare for tea by following the stepping stones around to the *tsukubai* (crouching basin), where they wash their mouths and hands. This is more of an ablution ceremony than actual washing. The *tsukubai* usually consists of a stone basin that has been placed in a low position, a front stone (*mae-ishi*), to stand on, a ring of stones in the center of which is a drain for water overflowing the basin, a *kakehi* arrangement for bringing water to the basin, a candlestick stone (*teshoku-ishi*) and hot water stone (*yuto-ishi*), placed left and right respectively, and a mirror stone (*kagami-ishi*), larger than everything else. A stone lantern is incorporated behind the *tsukubai* slightly to the left or right. The lanterns are placed to shed light on the basin and to guide the hands in washing.

On the way from the *tsukubai* to the teahouse, the guest will notice a small hole in the ground near the entrance, tucked back under the eaves. This is the *chiriana*, a "garbage pail" elevated to the level of abstract expression. Usually far too small to actually hold debris, it is made in a square or round shape and contains a *nozoki-ishi* that breaks up the geometry. The *chiriana* is ostensibly used for the trash picked up from the garden before the guests arrive. But rather than trash, one usually finds only a small branch or leaves, plus a pair of chopsticks called *chiribashi*, used for plucking debris from the garden. These will be placed to indicate that the garden has been cleaned in honor of the guests' arrival.

One may also encounter a small stone with some *shuronawa* rope tied around it, sitting on one of the *tobi-ishi* paths. This is a barrier-keeping stone (*sekimori-ishi*), another symbolic object usually found only in tea gardens, indicating that the visitor may not travel beyond this point.

As the guest approaches the teahouse, the last two or so stepping stones will rise slightly, leading to the large *kutsunugi-ishi* in front of the entrance to the teahouse. This is half the height from the

The *kutsunugi-ishi* and the entrance to the teahouse. Notice the *sekimori-ishi* and *chiriana*.

ground level to the entrance and broader than a stepping stone. My layout of the *nobedan* and stepping stones was calculated to give the longest path possible in this small space. Walking through the *roji*, the guest should have time to shake off daily life and enter the teahouse with an unencumbered heart and mind.

The entrance to the teahouse is quite low and is a defining feature of the *soan* or *koma* style expounded by Sen no Rikyu. The significance of this 29.5 x 29.5-inch (75 x 75-cm) *nijiriguchi* is that it forces anyone who comes through it to crawl into the space on hands and knees; another symbolic act in a ritual steeped in symbolism.

Finally, I want to draw attention to the choice of plants in the tea garden. These are restricted to plants without a strong scent and without large flowers—though small flowers are acceptable. I put to good use some of the trees remaining from the previously demolished garden, one of which was a shapely old pine. In addition, we added a number of dark-leafed shrubs such as *Ilex integra* (*mochi no ki*), *Ternstroemia gymnanthera* (*mokoku*), Japanese andromeda (*asebi*), *Eurya japonica* (*hisakaki*), as well as *Osmunda japonica* (*zenmai*), and haircap moss (*sugigoke*).

It is taught that the tea garden, like the teahouse, should be made in an unpretentious manner but with great care. The garden, though deceptively humble, might make use of unusual material, rare and ancient objects, or a collection of stones that are considered precious. Strive to make your tea garden with humility and a sense of joy.

The view from inside the teahouse. Notice the size of the entrance in relation to the window.

A mountain abode, in the middle of the city.

TOP: The entrance to the inner *roji* through the *yotsume gaki*.
BOTTOM: The deep eaves keep the area around the teahouse dry, even in the rainy season.

■ Backyard Tea Garden of the Yasushi Hokari Residence

The Hokari teahouse is nestled between the L-shaped residence (on the right in the photo above), the neighbor's house, and an old-style storehouse in the back. It is built as an extension to the residence. The tea garden is separated into inner and outer *roji* by a *yotsume gaki* fence. The outer *roji* serves as a backyard garden for the house as well. Stepping stones were placed leading to the teahouse and crossing the tea garden between the house and the frequently used storehouse.

Teahouses can be classified by size. *Koma* teahouses, with sizes of four-and-a-half *tatami* mats or less, are traditionally built in the *soan* style. This is a very rustic style with a *wara* (rice straw) roof, low ceiling, low *nijiriguchi*, a small *tokonoma,* and small windows for light only. The interior of the teahouse is calculated to prevent distractions so that the host may make tea with his whole heart, and so that the host and guests may focus all their attention on one another undisturbed. This was the style most advocated by Sen no Rikyu and his *wabi-cha* tea style. Anything larger than four-and-a-half mats is considered a *hiroma*.

A *hiroma* is usually constructed in a more open style with a wood or tile roofing, a higher ceiling, both low *nijiriguchi* and regular-height *kiniguchi*, larger windows for viewing the garden, larger *tokonoma*, and a generally more relaxed feeling.

Though only four-and-a-half mats large, this teahouse is a hybrid in that it is entered crawling, through a *nijiriguchi*, or upright, through a *kiniguchi*. This teahouse has a copper-tile roof and an additional deep eave on two sides (*hisashi*) that makes it feel much bigger. Especially when sitting inside with the doors removed, it feels almost like a gazebo (*azuma*). In addition to the room for serving tea, almost all teahouses have an additional one-half to two-mat *tokonoma* and a one- or two-mat room for preparation and cleanup called simply a water room (*mizuya*). This room contains at the very minimum a sink, a source of water, and a place for holding utensils. The *mizuya* and *tokonoma* space are not included in the calculation of floor space (i.e., 4.5 *tatami* mats only includes the space for guests to sit in).

The difference in gardens for these teahouses is generally one of scale, with stepping stones, water basin, etc., being a bit smaller for the *koma* teahouse and larger for the *hiroma*. Either type may be made in a formal, semiformal, or informal style.

The *yotsume gaki* is most often used in the tea garden because of its rustic appearance. This is often exaggerated by using bamboo with parts of the branches still attached. Structurally, it is the simplest of bamboo fences, with narrow vertical and horizontal members tied with *shuronawa* rope. But making one that looks handsome is not as easy as it looks, since it depends on subtleties of the dimensions, thickness of the bamboo poles, and spacing between the poles. It is a good idea to try two or three different versions on the spot, building a yard or two (1 to 2 m) of each before deciding on one (and you will need to hone your knot-tying skills!).

It has always been said about teahouses and tea gardens that they should "depict a mountain abode" and that one must strive to create the placid atmosphere of a cottage deep in the mountains, even though the garden may actually be in the midst of the city. For this garden I borrowed a technique from the *Izumo* style of garden making—one that I often use—spreading sand, dry-landscape style, in a tea garden. For the basin arrangement, a small replica of the double-measuring box (*niju masugata*) basin at Katsura Rikyu was used, and the lantern is in a slim and simple octagonal style.

A tea garden is ordinarily planted with broadleaf evergreen trees and shrubs. Unfortunately, most of these will not thrive in the region of Japan where this garden is located. Instead, the garden was composed largely with deciduous trees. This has made it distinctly different from a Kyoto tea garden, but I think that is just as well. It is a tea garden, radiant in green and particularly stunning in its autumn colors. Now, some dozen years since completion, with the trees grown out, the garden is evolving into the very image of a mountain abode.

The *yotsume gaki* makes for a very transparent demarcation of space.

With the doors of the teahouse removed, a gazebo-like atmosphere emerges.

The tea garden in winter.

HARMONIOUS BLEND OF JAPANESE AND WESTERN STYLE

Tsuneya Nakamura, former Seiko Epson Corp. president, wanted three different garden styles in different areas around his home. As he had appreciated my work on a previous tree garden, I proposed the same style for the approach garden. The main garden facing the house—a Western-style lawn garden with a pond—already existed and was to be left largely intact at the owner's request. The area around a new teahouse/guest house would be in a tea garden style; a sequence of Japanese to Western to Japanese. The three gardens would need to be seamlessly interconnected to form a harmonious whole.

This concept, in a small way, is similar to the stroll gardens (*kaiyu-shiki teien*) of the past, where one seemingly natural scene is juxtaposed with another equally natural but unrelated scene. These gardens actually grew out of large country estates, like Katsura Rikyu, which were made up of a main building and a number of small buildings, scattered throughout the landscape, as rest houses (including teahouses) and guest houses. The pleasure was simply in strolling through the gardens, passing famous symbolic scenes from Japan and China, resting at various teahouses, and returning home.

In terms of design, materials, and scale, this garden is more closely related to the early-Modern-era estates of the new industrial class that built combinations of Western-style and Japanese-style houses with gardens that combined aspects of both. Two outcomes of this fusion were the increase in open lawn spaces covered with grass, and the greater use of deciduous trees in the Japanese garden.

LEFT: A harmonious combination of Western-style lawn garden and Japanese-style tree garden with *sukiya*-style guest house. ABOVE: Room with a view: looking out from the *tatami*-matted guest house.

Multiple views of the garden presented by the flexible positioning of sliding *shoji* screens.

■ THEME, LAYOUT, AND ELEMENTS

When incorporating an existing garden into a larger design, as in this garden, you must think very carefully about how to make the best use of what already exists. I managed to create a dialogue between Japanese and Western design by the technique of incorporating a long *nobedan* in two staggered parts, so that the staggered point coincides with the existing rectangular pond. The boldly laid pavement serves to organically link the Japanese gardens in the front and rear, while joining in the centrality of the Western-style garden. Its geometric form echoes that of the pond but adds an informal texture. This texture was carried through to a new patio built adjacent to the pond and a glass-walled audio room.

As I mentioned, the approach to the main house was made into a tree garden. In this region, deciduous trees—such as the Japanese maple, trident maple, Japanese apricot, and Japanese stewartia—were never used in their natural shapes until the latter half of the twentieth century. In other words, even when using deciduous trees, they were trimmed in tiered and round shapes or bonsai-like forms. Evergreens were also trimmed into artificial shapes like tapered cones. Natural tree shapes were thought to run counter to the Japanese gardening aesthetic and were viewed unfavorably by many. This began to change around the late Modern era, partly as a result of the efforts of Aritomo Yamagata, "Ueji," Iida Juki, Kenzo Ogata, Saichi Kojima, and others who created major works involving "non-garden" trees. This type of garden became fully recognized as a garden style in the Postwar era.

The L-shaped pathway to the front door was made in *araidashi* (pebbled mortar),

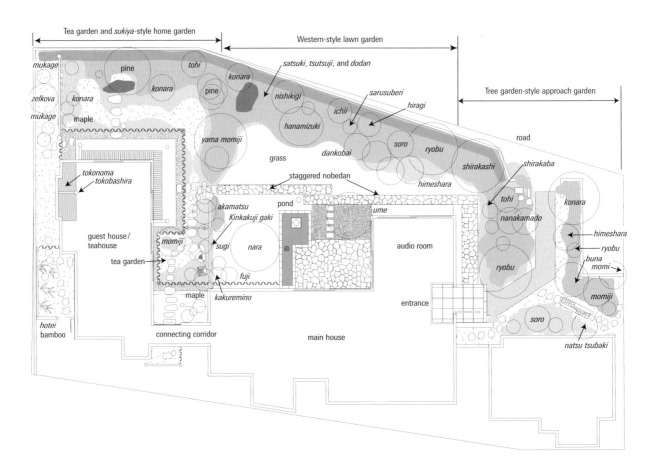

using brown gravel. A small *gyo*-style *nobedan* leads to the parking space. Both pathways leads people through a thicket of deciduous trees such as *Stewartia pseudo-camellia* (*natsu tsubaki*), Japanese beech (*buna*), white birch (*shirakaba*), and Japanese maple (*momiji*), and some evergreen trees such as *Abies firma* (*momi*) and *Quercus myrsinaefolia* (*shirakashi*) as they approach the front door. These trees are naturally shaped, and arranged to give this entrance garden a subtle charm.

Turning from the entrance, a walkway leads around the side of the house to the main gardens. As one rounds the main house the eye settles on the long, staggered, *nobedan* that carries the gaze immediately to the *sukiya*-style guest house at the rear of the property, giving a sense that this is the eventual end of the "journey." But following the *nobedan* leads first to the widening lawn garden and the square pond tucked behind the audio room. Here is an entrance to the back of the main house and a patio area where one can rest and take in the surrounding scene. Continuing on, one comes to the *sukiya*-style guest house that is also used for the tea ceremony. I had a *nure-en*—built like a *koshikake machiai* by adding clay walls at both ends—added around the *tatami*-matted living room space. It should be noted that *tatami* rooms serve a multiple function as living and sleeping space with the addition of futon bedding. The position of the *nobedan* coincides exactly with the *tokobashira* (a decorative post usually found at one end of the *tokonoma*), at the far end of the room facing the garden. I masked the guest house by creating peninsulas jutting out in front of it from right and left. I planted a large, well-shaped red pine on the left of the *nobedan* (when looking toward the building) and a large *yama momiji* to the

View of the rear garden from the guest house.

View from the rear garden of the guest house, toward the main house.

Looking toward the entrance from the car park.

right. The peninsulas were composed of shaped azalea on the right combined with a low *Kinkakuji gaki* fence to the left such that the *nobedan* just leads through this narrow gap. The large, shaped azalea and trees planted on the right completely shield the back part of the *sukiya*-style guest house from view, creating an intimate but open area. To the left side of the building, another intimate garden is formed in the area between the main house, the guest house, and the corridor that connects them. This recalls classic Japanese "pavilion"-style construction that was typical of *shinden*-style architecture. Here was the perfect opportunity for a small, informal tea garden. This garden consists of some large stepping stones, *Oribe*-style lantern, and a *tsukubai* with a basin made from the inverted shade of a stone lantern, with a square hole cut into it. The tea garden is separated from the lawn garden by the low, *Kinkakuji*-style bamboo fence.

I believe the reason this unusual garden was successful is because it is a garden free of stereotypes. Geometric and natural forms, Western and Japanese styles, deciduous and evergreen trees—all live in harmony, each keeping their identity while offering their own particular beauty to the whole.

The entrance to the main house: a passage through a forest grove.

▶ A tea garden atmosphere created in the small space between guest house and main house.

The view of the pond and tree and lawn garden, from the audio room.

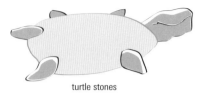

turtle stones

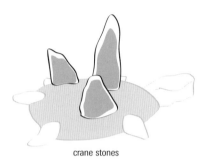

crane stones

CONSTRUCTING A BASIC CRANE-AND-TURTLE ISLAND

Turtle islands have been made in Japanese gardens since ancient times. An ancient Chinese legend tells that somewhere in the East China Sea is an island called Penglai ("Horai" in Japanese), abounding with the elixir of life and carried on the back of an enormous turtle. This legend spread to Japan, where it was incorporated into gardens. Over the ages a number of auspicious themes were worked into the fabric of the turtle-island myth. Between the Medieval and Modern eras in particular, a crane theme was added and many crane-and-turtle gardens were made across Japan. Both crane and turtle carry the symbolism of longevity and good fortune.

As with waterfalls, the shape and size of turtle islands has changed over the generations. In older periods, the island was larger in relation to the pond size and the turtle's features were often difficult to discern. Toward the end of the Pre-modern era, we see islands getting smaller and more clearly defined. The height of the head changes from older gardens—exhibiting heads that are held aloft—to later designs in which the head drops lower until it seems half submerged. Here I will outline the creation of a combination crane-and-turtle island that I constructed—along with a dry garden—in the courtyard of a Buddhist temple:

In a small garden, a single island embodies both turtle and crane themes.

1. The ground is leveled and made as flat as possible. This is done in relation to the level of the *nure-en* and floor level inside the building.

2. Decide the direction that the head of the turtle will face. In this case the garden is in a Jodo Buddhist temple—a sect of Buddhism that reveres the "Western Paradise"—so the head of the turtle faces west. In ponds with waterfalls, the head of the turtle will often face the waterfall.

3. Decide the size of the island in relation to the size of the garden. With a small garden such as this one, the island too will be small, about 3.2 yards (3 m) in diameter. Height is also related to size but in any case should be fairly low. This island is about 20 inches (50 cm) high, not including the stones.

A large expanse of granite sand gives the island the appearance of floating.

4. Pile and shape the soil into a slightly elliptical shape, then begin setting the stones for the head, tail, and four legs of the turtle.

5. The stone for the head is largest and set first. This should somewhat reflect the shape of a turtle head and should not be too jagged. The stone is set so that most of it juts out from the narrow end of the elliptical mound.

6. The stones for the legs are somewhat smaller and elongated. These are set lower than the height of the head and jut out only slightly from the mounded soil. The second-largest stone is that for the tail. It too should be elongated and set at the end of the island opposite the head, jutting out from the mounded soil.

7. Next we set the stone for the neck of the crane and, as this image would dictate, this is a tall, slender, and somewhat jagged stone. This stone needs to be well buried so as not to become unstable.

8. Next come the "wing" and "tail" stones, which should be a half to one third the height of the neck but also slender and jagged. These stones should be broader at the base than that for the neck, as would be appropriate for the image. They are set on either side and somewhat behind the neck stone.

9. After the stones are set, a tree is planted on the island. Traditionally, this is a twisted old pine tree, kept small by pruning. The crane, the turtle, and the pine are all symbols of longevity. However, in this case we used a twisted old maple that existed on the site. This added some color to an otherwise austere garden. The tree will be kept small through pruning.

10. Finally, haircap moss is planted over the mounded soil to complete the island.

In following themes such as this one, avoid applying images too rigidly. The main idea of the turtle is the expression of age, like an old mountain worn down by time. The crane expresses age in terms of renewal and therefore its stones are angular and reach upward. While the turtle image pictured here is rather explicit, creating a literal image is not the goal.

A restored waterfall and pond from the Pre-modern era.

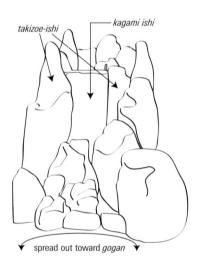

takizoe-ishi *kagami ishi*

spread out toward *gogan*

The restored lower fall of a three-fall setting.

RESTORATION OF A WATERFALL AND *GOGAN* SETTING

Although the name of this temple, *Gokuraku* (Western Paradise), is normally associated with the Jodo sect of Buddhism, this is a garden in a mountainside Zen temple. Its pond garden has been preserved for ages though it has been repaired many times. Although neither the exact date of its making nor the name of its creator is known, forms and techniques dating to the beginning or middle of the Pre-modern era could be observed.

The garden needed repair on a sweeping scale. Stones had moved over the ages, and everything had grown discordant after so many repairs and adjustments. It was totally overgrown with *tamamono* shrubs and shaped trees. With the exception of the waterfall grouping at the very back and part of the turtle island, the garden had become a far cry from what it originally was. The location of the three-tiered waterfall and the sizes of the pond and the turtle island appeared not to have changed, so it was decided that only the pond edge (*gogan*) setting and other stone groupings, including the lower waterfall, needed full repair and restoration.

The style and techniques of a Japanese garden vary from age to age, and any very old garden has been handled by many owners and gardeners of different tastes and skills. From the Heian (794–1185) to the Kamakura (1185–1333) periods, for example, waterfalls were not made very tall, usually only 12 inches (30 cm) to 1 yard (1 m). From Kamakura on, the influence of Chinese Zen monks and Chinese ink painting had an impact on waterfall making. Tall waterfalls became the rule, especially in mountain temples. The waterfall in Tenryuji is about 11 yards (10 m) tall, and Kinkakuji has a waterfall of about 2.1 yards (2 m) in height. At the same time, three-tiered waterfalls (the same as in this garden) and so-called "dragon-gate" (*ryumon*) falls became commonplace. In general, stone groupings and settings were taller and more angular from the Kamakura period on. But by the end of the Pre-modern era, stones had become rounder, flatter, and set more horizontally than vertically, a trend that continues to this day. It is difficult to account for the change, but it may be related to experience with tall settings falling over in earthquakes, an increasing lack of larger stones, or a decline in the influence of Zen and Chinese culture. Because the Pre-modern era spanned more than two and a half centuries, gardens made in the early years are naturally quite different from those made in the final years. I did my best to mend the pond and waterfall based on techniques of the early Pre-modern era. Concrete was not known then, so almost everything was done with clay and stone. Plaster was sometimes used to set the stones around the pond and in *nobedan* walkways, but we did not follow this practice—which seems to have been an expedient—because it is not durable. Stone settings in this period were more vertical and jagged, and this is the style we followed.

In this region, where temperatures drop to minus 10 degrees Celsius for several weeks each year, stones need to be refastened—such as by repacking the clay around the stones—every few years. Even concrete will not hold the stones in place indefinitely. The best thing to do is bury the stones as deeply as possible and to use careful setting techniques and only packed clay and stone so that it is easier to carry out inevitable repairs in the future.

Although we were repairing a waterfall and pond stone setting (*gogan*), making these settings from scratch will follow the same general order outlined here:

1. Starting from the waterfall, we will gradually move down to the edge of the pond, setting the stones as we go. You will need to have all the stones on site before

A restored *gogan* and pond from the Edo period.

you start. A rough sketch of each actual stone and the intended setting should be made. The important thing in this sketch is the relative size and the intended orientation of each stone. Think about how the stones will fit against each other and have extra stones on site in case of problems or last-minute changes.

2. Begin the waterfall by shaping the area with soil. The soil is piled up and dug out for each stone, rather than placing the stone then piling dirt around it. With very large settings, a supporting structure of concrete is made first. Start with the middle stone (called the mirror stone or *kagami-ishi*) by standing it straight and leaning it slightly forward with the flat face out. The bottom end should be buried as deeply as possible and the flat top edge should be level. When the stone is buried, the soil around it is tamped down with a wood pole to be sure there are no gaps. The stone used here is about 2.1 yards (2 m) x 35.4 inches (90 cm) wide and 8 inches (20 cm) thick.

3. Immediately after the *kagami-ishi*, you want to place the supporting stones (*takizoe-ishi*) to the left or right front side. This stone supports the *kagami-ishi* and should lean back against it and in toward its center. Again, bury this sufficiently to hold both stones in place.

The overgrown pond and island (above) and the restored setting (facing page).

4. Place the next *takizoe-ishi* on the other side of the *kagami-ishi*. Both *takizoe-ishi* should be taller than the *kagami-ishi* to funnel the falling water. If such large stones are not available, it is possible to lay shorter stones at the base and set stones above that to gain the height. In that case, mask the joint by placing another stone in front of that assembly, giving the impression that the *takizoe-ishi* is larger than it really is. Continue placing stones to the right-front and left-front until the waterfall is complete. Test the flow of water over the falls and check for leaks.

5. The bottom of the falls will spread out to join the *gogan* setting around the pond. Several rules of thumb about this setting:

   • No stone at the pond edge should be taller than the waterfall itself.

   • The stones must be buried or supported sufficiently so that they will not move.

   • Keep in mind that the purpose of the stones is to keep the surrounding dirt out of the pond and project a rugged, natural image. The stones will need to be at least slightly above the level of the surrounding soil surface.

   • The stones closer to the waterfall are generally larger or more vertical, getting smaller or more horizontal at the edge of the pond closest to the house or furthest from the waterfall. Be careful to avoid symmetry between the left and right sides.

   • The edge of the pond should turn in toward the center, then out again to produce a meandering, non-geometric edge. Likewise, the heights of the stones rise and fall to form a pleasing visual rhythm.

   • Stones should overlap each other or butt against each other tightly so as to keep water from seeping through. Notching stone is acceptable to insure this, so long as the cut areas do not show. If concrete is poured to form the pond and edge, this becomes less critical.

   • Stones should be set so that the pond-side face is standing straight up or

leaning slightly in the direction of the pond. Don't lean your stones away from the center or produce the effect of an opening flower.

- Be very careful to compact the clay under and around the stones. Any gaps will quickly fill with water, resulting in the pond leaking or the stone moving after a short time.

- Be careful when planting trees behind the stone. Be sure to leave sufficient space for growth between the trunk of the tree and the nearest stone. If you start with the tree leaning against the stone, as the tree grows, it may push the stone into the pond.

- All *gogan* settings tend to be a bit hard and rough in appearance. To soften this appearance, add some flatter and rounder stones, especially on the side of the pond closest to the house.

- Different effects can be gained later on by planting shrubs or ground cover around the edge of the pond. This will also help soften the edge, but be careful not to let these plants overtake the stones entirely in the future, as happened before at Gokurakuji.

- A broad, flat stone is often incorporated into the near side of the *gogan*, allowing visitors to come close to the edge of the pond.

Two final points: in the case of a three-tiered waterfall such as this, trees should not be planted around the lowest waterfall to the extent that they entirely block the view of the two waterfalls further back. In such settings, it is not uncommon to find a *sanzon seki* (three-Buddha) stone arrangement at the very back behind or sometimes comprising the first fall.

It is also common in ponds of the Pre-modern era to find a *"horai ganto"* stone sticking up from the pond somewhere close to the foreground. Symbolically, this stone points back toward the falls, and visually it adds depth to the view from the building side.

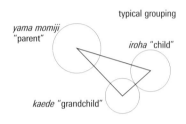

yama momiji

iroha

kaede

typical grouping by type and size

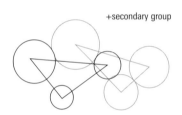

typical grouping

yama momiji
"parent"

iroha "child"

kaede "grandchild"

+secondary group

first group

secondary group

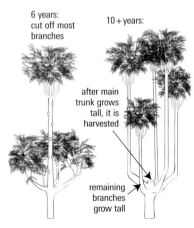

6 years:
cut off most
branches

10 + years:

after main
trunk grows
tall, it is
harvested

remaining
branches
grow tall

Daisugi

PLANTING AND ARRANGING GARDEN TREES

As I mentioned in Chapter 1, trees considered suitable for the garden (*niwaki*) consisted mostly of broadleaf and coniferous evergreens. Though deciduous trees such as the willow, apricot, and cherry have always been used, gardens composed primarily of deciduous trees were unheard of. In Nagano, where I do much of my work, the dry and cold climate severely restricts the variety of trees we can use. That is why deciduous trees play such an important role in many of my gardens. I expect the same is true in many parts of the world.

In planting trees, a simple approach is to think in terms of grouping sizes and grouping species. In composing a group of trees, it is helpful to think in terms of threes. A typical group of trees should include large, medium, and small in terms of the height of the tree. For home gardens, a maximum height of 5.4 yards (5 m) is good for a two- to three-story house. This puts the tallest tree near the roof height. A tree of 5.4 yards (5 m), one of 3.2 yards (3 m) and one of 2.1 yards (2 m) would be a typical group. The trees should be grouped at the points of an irregular triangle with the largest tree at the backmost corner. Think in terms of the largest tree scattering seed that is carried on the wind. A newer (and therefore smaller) tree grows within this area and it too scatters seed that produces a tree. To increase the volume of the group, add more groupings of three.

The trees in the group should belong to roughly the same species. Mixing unrelated species in the same group is one of the main causes of deciduous tree gardens looking like nurseries. Within a group, for example, a *yama momiji* will grow largest, an *iroha momiji* several yards less and a *hauchiwa kaede* less than that. This grouping gives a natural appearance while having enough variety of color and leaf to be interesting.

Trees cast shadows. Arrange your trees so that they all receive proper light, or select smaller trees that require half-shaded areas and place them in the shadow of the larger trees. If trees that you anticipated to stay small grow tall and ruin your composition, it may be necessary to replace or cut them back. For example, a multiple-trunk *momiji* may start with all the trunks relatively the same thickness, but after five years, one of the trunks may have far surpassed the others. In that case you can cut the trunk somewhere within a yard (1 m) of the ground. New shoots will grow up around the periphery and you can trim some of these back while allowing others to grow. When another trunk grows too wide, you can repeat the process indefinitely. Generally speaking, with deciduous trees, we are interested in natural shapes and minimal maintenance. Depending on the tree, we are concerned mostly with dead branch removal and occasional thinning.

Although I speak a lot about deciduous trees in this book, even gardens dominated by such trees employ lots of evergreens. For blocking unwanted views, as wind breaks, as hedges (*ikegaki*), or just to enjoy greenery all year round, broadleaf evergreens, pines, and conifers are an indispensable part of the Japanese garden.

■ A Note on *Daisugi*

This tree has a long history in Japanese architecture. Growers in the Kitayama area of Kyoto began to cultivate trees for maximum harvest, as far back as the Muromachi period (1392–1573). Branches of the tree are all trimmed off except for the very upper and lower branches. This promotes growth of the trunk. When the tree has reached a maximum height, the main trunk is cut and used for the columns of buildings. The branches around the stump are pruned to leave only the most promising. These shoots also grow vertical and straight, and the resulting narrower poles are then used as ceiling rafters. From sometime in the Meiji period (1868–1912), this radically cut tree began to appear in the garden. It can take between ten and twenty years to reach a condition suitable for use as a feature tree.

From the point of view of the garden, some positive points about this tree are that it has a straight, vertical profile good for narrow spaces. It doesn't cast a lot of shadow and the foliage is compacted in tufts that appear to have been shaped but are natural.

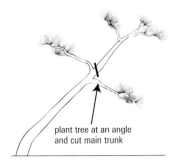

plant tree at an angle and cut main trunk

■ A Note on the *Mon Kaburi* (Gate-Shading) Black Pine

The practice of planting a tree at the entrance gate of the property dates from the Classical era. Often such trees carried symbolic or geomantic meaning. One tree that has been used in this way—at least since the Pre-modern era—is the pine. The tree is shaped so that one branch hangs over the gate and is therefore called a *mon kaburi* (gate-covering or gate-shading) pine.

There are basically two important aspects to this tree: creating a curving shape, and promoting the length and horizontality of the first branch. To achieve this, the tree is planted at an angle from a young age. When the tree is still young (1 to 1.6 yards/1 to 1.5 m tall) the main trunk is cut at a point where there is a solid branch facing upward. This causes the branch to become the main trunk, and it is encouraged to grow vertically by tying it to bamboo poles. The closest downward-facing branch on the opposite side is also tied to a bamboo pole to tilt it at an angle slightly less than horizontal. It is encouraged to grow by cutting off the branches below it. The height of this first branch should eventually be about 2.1 yards (2 m) from the base of the tree, in order to "cover" the entrance gate where it will be installed. This is the basic shape, but an S shape is often formed by again cutting the top of the new trunk, this time promoting the branch on the downward side to become the new trunk. Here it can be left to grow naturally, or it can continue to be bent and twisted into a spiraling S by selective cutting and tying. A key point is to cut off branches on the concave side of the bend while shaping those on the convex side.

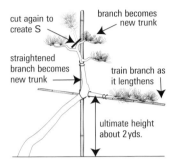

cut again to create S

branch becomes new trunk

straightened branch becomes new trunk

train branch as it lengthens

ultimate height about 2 yds.

mon kaburi

■ Using and Maintaining Moss

Moss is used more extensively in the Japanese garden than anywhere else in the world. Like many Japanese garden conventions, this too has its roots in Kyoto, where moss grows easily and abundantly. Though there are thousands of different types of moss, the one I use most often is *sugigoke*, called haircap or haircup moss. When flourishing, this moss creates a thick, fluffy carpet that will even need trimming. Generally, though, it is somewhat temperamental and easily becomes patchy or dies if conditions are not right. Those conditions consist of, first of all, a soil that retains moisture well, drains quickly, and is fairly acidic. We usually use *yamazuna*, a mix of red clay and sand, when planting moss.

Next is moisture in the air. Humid conditions are ideal for moss and dry conditions will kill it faster than anything else. Moss does not have a true root system and relies on airborne moisture. Conversely, over-watering and leaf buildup above the moss can cause it to rot in wet or humid conditions. Ideally, a fine mist should be sprayed into the air above the moss. In recent years I have begun to use a mister, placed at the

New moss, purchased in mats, much like turf.

A mister used to saturate the air over the garden area.

first-floor roof level and facing the garden. I run the mister for several minutes in the morning and several minutes at night, with adjustments for summer and winter. After several seasons the results have been good.

When a patch does burn or dry out, remove it and replace it with fresh material. Spare moss should be kept close by to quickly replace dead patches with material that has grown up in the same environment. With so many varieties of moss available, the best assurance of survival is to use moss that you find already growing in the immediate area of your garden.

HANDLING STONE

As with bamboo, stone is used extensively throughout the Japanese garden. Here I will outline some aspects of stone handling.

Stone is either discovered on the site—as the remains of an old garden or excavated when a new building is being made—or purchased from suppliers. When decorative stone is shipped by truck, it needs to be protected to avoid scratching and chipping. If the stone is not onsite already, getting it onsite will be your first task. When stone is moved around by crane, a heavy fabric or rope sling is used to avoid scratching the surface. Depending on the size of the stone and the size of the garden, a small backhoe can be fitted with a sling for lifting and moving stones in tight spaces. We sometimes use a small crane that we call a crab because the size of the machine (about 35 inches/90 cm wide) allows it to get through very tight spaces, but the legs can be extended 2.1 yards (2 m) on each side. This allows lifting jobs up to 1.5 tons. However, very large stones may weigh between 3 and 5 tons.

When it is impossible to use a crane or backhoe, traditional methods need to be employed. The simplest of these is to create a roller and sled arrangement. A sled built of heavy timber, at least 4 inches (10 cm) square, is assembled in a simple frame.

A small crane called a crab.

A sled loaded with stone and pulled across PVC pipes.

A *sanmatta* and chain block lifting a stone into place.

CLOCKWISE FROM TOP LEFT: Using a diamond wheel cutter to begin the cut in a slab of granite. Rapping the *koyasuke* with a sledgehammer. The rough-cut stone.

Lay flat and wide wooden rails along the ground leading to where the stone will be deposited. Short lengths of PVC or steel pipe are laid perpendicular across the rails and the sled is placed on top of these. The stone is lifted onto the sled and the sled is pulled and pushed across the pipe. Keep displacing the pipe from the back to the front of the sled. This technique is primitive but effective.

When setting the stone, lifting without a crane means setting up a tripod (*sanmatta*) with a chain block attached to the top. This tripod is made from 3.2-yard (3-m) long, 4-inch (10-cm) diameter poles bound together with heavy wire at the top. The ends of the poles are dug into the ground or anchored with stakes. The chain block is hung from the wire. Again, a fabric or rope sling is used around the stone, and the stone should be as close to the hole dug for it as possible. Be careful, as the stone starts to lift and swing toward the center of the tripod, which should be set directly over the hole. The operation requires two to three people plus another person to look at how the stone is being placed, checking it from the main viewing position and then from all sides. Stones up to about three tons can be lifted with the *sanmatta*. When the stone is lowered, put some smaller stones underneath it to allow the sling to be pulled out.

This type of system can also be used for lifting stones higher than ground level—for waterfalls or stones on slopes. This operation requires some experience and a lot of hands. It involves setting the tripod close to the slope, raising the stone to the maximum height, and removing one leg while firmly holding the tripod with ropes from several angles. This bipod is allowed to fall slowly toward the slope until the stone comes to rest. The tripod is then reconstructed further up the slope and the stone pulled up again.

When we speak about stone in the Japanese garden we are talking about the relatively narrow range of types listed below (left).

In addition to large stones, many are also used in the form of pebbles and cobbles, the most desirable of these being black, naturally rounded river stones called *nachiguro*.

For working stone, there are a limited number of tools, listed below (right).

STONES	
Ao-ishi	Hard blue-green schist with streaks of white. Highly prized stone for all types of stone settings. Also found in red, purple, and other shades.
Anzan gan	A blackish andesite, volcanic stone ranging from hard to soft, used for all types of stone settings.
Sado-ishi	Named after Sado island, where it is found. Similar to *ao-ishi* but usually in reddish tones. New stone is no longer available.
Granite	The mainstay of the Japanese garden, used for settings and all kinds of objects from lanterns to basins, walls, stairs, and stepping stones.
Kurama-ishi	Most often used for stepping stones, a granite from Mount Kurama and Yamanashi prefecture (also called *Koshu kurama*) that contains iron, giving the stone its characteristic rust to blackish color.
Teppei-seki	Slate used for stepping stones and walkways, wall, and roof surfacing, and sometimes in river settings.

TOOLS	
Chisel and sledgehammer	For chipping, shaping, and breaking stones.
Diamond wheel-cutter	For making straight cuts or jagged cuts when used together with the chisel and sledgehammer.
Impact drill	For making holes.
Koyasuke	A kind of sledgehammer with a broad, blunt carbide edge, used for making straight chips on the corners or edges of slabs or splitting. It is used by hitting it on the back end with a small sledgehammer.
Seto or *ryoto*	Another heavy hammer with a broad, chisel-like edge on both ends, used for chipping out a shape in stone.
Stiff-bristle (brass) brushes	For cleaning stone.

Interior and Veranda Gardens in Commercial Spaces

A GARDEN OF LARGE-SCALE BONSAI

The old wooden inn of Hamanoyu was to be torn down and rebuilt as a twelve-story hotel with a traditional flavor. Gardens play a critical role in a Japanese-style hotel. I was therefore brought onto the project team at the earliest stages. I built ten gardens during the final phase of building construction with only one month in which to do it. Most of them had to be built into the architecture in one form or another, being either indoors, on roofs, or on verandas. The foremost issue when making an indoor garden is how to maintain the essentials—water, airborne moisture, temperature, light, and soil—in a state conducive to plant growth. To prepare for the Hamanoyu project, I toured various indoor gardens in the Tokyo area and searched for source material. In the end, I turned to my experience with bonsai to develop the main theme of the gardens in Hamanoyu.

Of the ten gardens we built for this hotel, I will highlight two of the largest ones and one typical veranda type in this chapter. Although a project of this scale and difficulty is not something I would recommend to try for anyone but a seasoned professional, I include it in this book because of the increasing interest in and construction of gardens in interior spaces. I think the lessons I learned in the process can be of benefit even to apartment or restaurant owners and designers thinking of creating a natural-looking garden on a veranda, in a covered hotel lobby, or in a shopping mall. These gardens, which have been an integral part of the hotel's operation for more than twenty years, provide a good example of a Japanese-garden approach to this design problem.

THEME, LAYOUT, AND ELEMENTS

The basic theme of all the gardens in Hamanoyu is "a garden of large-scale bonsai." This is a design-driven theme based on two important factors. First, the growth of the roots is restricted by the architecture. This meant the shallow soil needed to retain water longer in order for the limited root system to absorb it adequately. Second, the drainage had to be excellent and the excess water could not be allowed to pool around the roots and rot them. It occurred to me that this was very similar to the conditions of bonsai and the idea formed the basis of my design decisions.

The two main gardens in Hamanoyu were on the second floor of a T-shaped, three-story pavilion, housing restaurants, clubs, and reception rooms, as well as the hotel lobby. The gardens were situated so that they could be enjoyed by guests seated in the *tatami*-matted dining rooms that overlook them. For the larger and longer of these two gardens, we decided to create a *yarimizu* or *kyokusui* (meandering stream) garden, with the stream terminating in a waterfall into the lobby below. In this way, guests

A river runs through it: private dining spaces
overlook an interior stream garden.

Protruding beams are covered with stone before creating the stream.

could enjoy the garden and stream atmosphere while eating and drinking—a scene not unlike that on the shores of the famous Kamo River in Kyoto.

Large, protruding beams from the structure below and their direction restricted the shape and placement of the stream. I managed to get the height of some of these beams reduced, but this was as far as the architect could go. I was more successful in influencing the amount of natural light coming into the space. At my request, not only was the glass area of the roof increased, but the upper section of the wall over the back end of the pavilion was changed to glass—allowing more light to penetrate the area.

The second garden on this level was made to the left of the main lobby—in one of the arms of the T—entirely separated from the stream garden. This space was to be in a tea-garden style, but the operators of the hotel wanted another stream and waterfall, this time cascading over the glass wall of the club below. Streams and ponds are not normally features of a tea garden, but then, there is nothing normal when it comes to bringing nature into an artificial environment. Here too I was able to influence the architecture to the extent of having much larger *nure-en* built than originally designed, and having deep eaves (*hisashi*) built over these. The result greatly improved the integration between interior space and tea garden for the rooms at that end of the pavilion.

When making indoor gardens or courtyard gardens in a new construction like this, nothing is more important than consultations with the architect and construction company. Unless the gardener can understand the limitations and possibilities offered

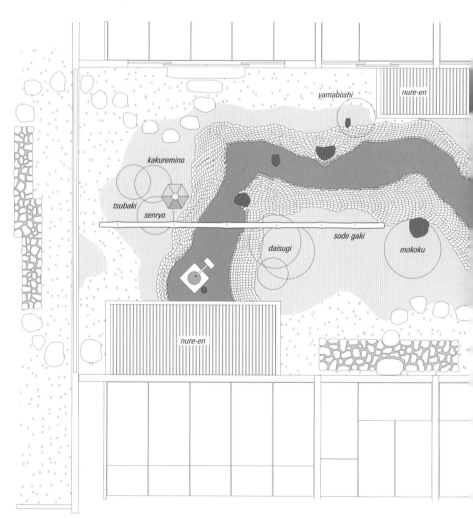

by the architecture, he cannot give the architect advice as to the proper positioning and use of *shoji* and other types of screening devices, placement and sizes of open verandas, and the proper balance between garden and architecture. Japanese gardens exhibit their full beauty only when they blend with the architecture. Indeed, I believe Japanese gardening boasts the highest level of garden-architecture integration in the world.

For most of the garden area, we originally had only a depth of 15.7 inches (40 cm) to work with for planting. Here too I worked with the architect to get a minimum of 27.5 inches (70 cm) in the main areas. Even so, extremely large trees were out of the question. I was, however, able to plant Japanese maples of up to 3.2 yards (3 m) in height.

Elements

Following the theme of "large-scale bonsai," the most important elements in this garden were the most basic, beginning with the soil. I discuss the composition of the soil later on in this chapter.

Light filtered through the ceiling glass and a diffusion grid was an element essential for the success of this garden.

Water in the form of a stream is the main feature of the large garden and a subtheme of the tea garden. Water in the form of vapor—or I should say, the lack of— was and continues to be an important element in Hamanoyu.

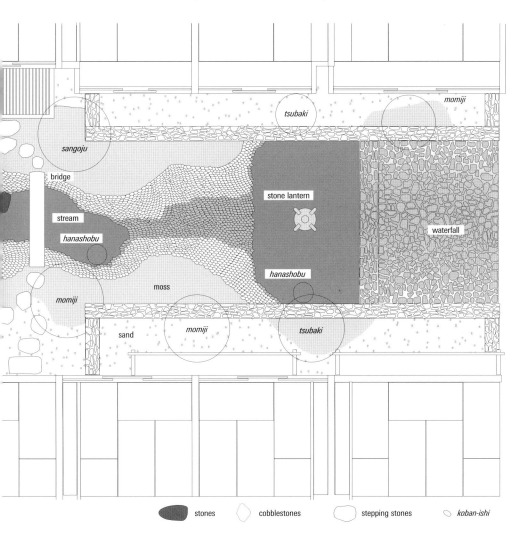

stones   ◇ cobblestones   ▢ stepping stones   ◌ *koban-ishi*

CREATING THE GARDEN

Obviously, with a garden created indoors and at the tail end of the construction of the building itself, planning, timing, and manpower take on a more important role. Our total construction schedule for ten separate gardens was just one month. We worked with a crew of about thirty men including the stonemasons, crane operator, and truck drivers. This meant working day and night, which, on the other hand, was somewhat more comfortable considering that we were indoors.

Before the exterior walls were completely sealed up, we had to make sure materials of any substantial weight or volume were on site. This often meant we were working with stocks of materials piled up around us. Architecture in areas already finished needed to be protected from dirt or marring, while in areas where construc-

The view across the stream.

The entrance lobby and waterfall, with a view of the stream garden on the second level.

tion was still going on, we had to contend with scaffolding and workers from other trades crisscrossing our work area. In other words, the natural progression of the work was completely disrupted.

As much as possible, we attempted to keep the construction procedure the same as any other garden. That means beginning with the soil. We used a mixture of five different soils that we blended ourselves. As there was no place to do this inside, it was done in the street outside and hauled up to the second floor with a power shovel, where it was dropped onto a conveyer. The conveyer was shifted every time an area became full, until most of the soil was in. The exceptions were areas where stonework had to be done before the soil could be placed or waterproofing of the underlying concrete was not yet finished. All the concrete must first be overlaid with waterproof sheeting—along with water outlets and inlets—but the construction contractor handled most of this work.

Once the soil was in, trees were planted. Most of the stonework, other than stepping stones, was for the stream and the waterfall, including surfacing the beams sticking up past the level of the garden floor. In some cases, *nobedan* stonework was done before the surrounding soil was in place by building a form and filling it to the proper level with dirt, mortar, and stone. This was because of the need to make progress on any area we could, regardless of the conditions. With the main stonework finished, all areas to be filled with soil were completed and stepping stones were placed. Finally, moss and sand and some elements like *sode gaki* and *chozubachi* were placed. Weight issues meant we could not set any large stones without entirely hollowing them out—a costly process. We therefore set only stones small enough to be lifted by two men.

Problems

Unfortunately, this work took place in winter. We learned the hard way that trees grown outdoors cannot survive the sudden increase in temperature—caused by being placed in a warm interior environment—when they would normally be in a dormant period. Due to the sudden change of temperature and atmosphere, a number of trees dried out and died within a month and had to be replaced.

The main cause of the trees dying was the heating/air conditioning system drying out the air. If the humidity drops to less than 50%, the leaves begin to dry out. Therefore they needed to be sprayed with water morning and night. Trees absorb and release an incredible amount of water each day under normal growth conditions, a process known as transpiration. Although we took the precaution of adding automatic misters in the ceiling area over the garden, continuous problems with clogging rendered them unusable. With one or two exceptions the trees need to be replanted every three to five years in order to keep a fresh appearance. A less problematic but unforeseen difference with planting indoors was that the leaves of trees like maples failed to change color or fall off by the second winter after planting.

Finally, insects lying dormant in the trees and plants suddenly sprang to life when transplanted from the winter to the warm indoor environment. The trees had to be sprayed—which solved the problem—but this was best done outdoors beforehand. In the end it would have been advisable to carry out the work in summer or transplant trees from greenhouses that had been cultivated in an environment similar to their new home.

One problem we did manage to avoid was that of foul odors produced by rotting soil and mold. Because we took such great care with soil mix and drainage, this common problem with moist indoor environments did not occur.

▶ A view of the entire length of the building showing the glass roof and balcony crossing the lobby.

Mixing soil in the street and lifting it to a conveyer.

The finished garden in early evening with lanterns lit outside the dining rooms.

CONSTRUCTING THE INDOOR STREAM GARDEN

There are two main aspects to this garden: the stream itself and the soil and plantings around it. In both cases the all-important point is how to deal with water in an interior space.

My first concern was the composition of the soil and the method of drainage. To this end, we first laid in a network of perforated PVC pipes to carry away excess water. These emptied out into the drains provided by the building contractor.

Over this we used a base of ¾ to 1¼-inch (2 to 3-cm) diameter perlite to a depth of 8 to 12 inches (20 to 30 cm). Perlite is an expanded, lightweight, siliceous rock. The perlite is essential both for drainage and weight reduction of the soil. Above the perlite we laid sheets of plastic mesh—the kind often sold with flowerpots to prevent soil from draining out the hole in the bottom—to keep the perlite from getting clogged with soil.

Above this we added a mix of the following soils:

Black soil	5 parts—nutrient rich
Kanuma	1 part—normally used for *satsuki* bonsai
Fuyodo	1 part—leafy soil with good moisture retention and nutrition
Akadama	1 part—general-purpose bonsai soil with excellent water retention
Fujizuna	1 part—general bonsai soil often used as a topsoil to retain heat but also retains its properties under freezing conditions

The *kanuma*, *akadama*, and *fujizuna* are all soils used in planting bonsai. As mentioned earlier, my theme for this garden was "large-scale bonsai." As with bonsai, water would be added to the plant from the top down and drained off quickly, and therefore is available to the roots for a much shorter time than in a normal planting. Bonsai soils are designed to allow good ventilation and hold moisture well so that restricted roots can have time to use it. Yet if pooled water is retained around the roots or air circulation is inadequate, they will quickly rot and the plant will die. The combination of these soils over a bed of perlite created excellent drainage and adequate moisture retention at the same time. Although bonsai never use black soil or *fuyodo*, these nutrient-rich soils are essential for the well-being of full-size trees.

The architect originally called for a depth of 15.7 inches (40 cm) for planting, but I insisted on 27.5 inches (70 cm) in order to plant trees of an appropriate size for the scale of the building. So above the 8 inches (20 cm) of perlite, we were able to lay in the bonsai soil mix by an additional 20 inches (50 cm). The root ball of a 3.2 to 4.3-yard (3 to 4-m) deciduous tree is roughly 20 inches (50 cm) in diameter.

After filling in the soil, we dug out the area for the stream to a depth of about 12 to 20 inches (30 to 50 cm) at the deepest part under the point where a bridge would be placed. We created as meandering a stream as possible, given that protruding beams from the underlying floor limited the area we had to work in. We put in a vinyl liner with 2 inches (5 cm) of mortar above that under the stream area.

On top of the mortar we laid in *koban-ishi*, a flat, oval stone about 4 to 6 inches (10 to 15 cm) diameter and ¾ to 2 inches (2 to 5 cm) thickness, in an overlapping "fish-scale" (*uroko*) pattern starting from the bottom of the stream wall and working to the top. Then large *Shirakawa* sand, about ⅜ to ⅗ inch (9 to 15 mm) in diameter, was laid in the bottom of the stream.

The stream is visible from a balcony that joins the left and right halves of the floor overlooking it. I wanted to place a stone bridge across the stream at a point that would look good from this view. The bridge was necessary to give the hotel staff a place to cross. For this bridge I wanted a very low profile and slight arch to harmonize with the open vista of the garden. This required the use of a cut stone rather than a naturally shaped one. In keeping with the low-slung profile of the bridge, we used no *hashibasami* stones to anchor it and no base stones to support it. Instead, we just notched the mortar to let the ends of the bridge sit down into the level of the surrounding soil.

Next, we brought in the trees and planted them after first digging out the soil. As this planting is over a concrete base, the roots need room to spread horizontally.

Stepping stones, *kutsunugi-ishi*, *nobedan*, and miscellaneous stones (*sute-ishi*) were then set.

The protruding beams on both sides were earlier covered with rough granite to give them the appearance of low retaining walls. The water for the stream emanates from three locations, the first at the very beginning—from under one of the extended wooden *nure-en*—the second from under the bridge. Just past the bridge, the stream runs down a slope to a deeper pool lined with a double layer of the same *koban-ishi* used for the stream. Here, another water source adds to the volume of water that cascades over the waterfall to the lobby below.

In this pool I fixed a *hisaki-gata* (or *rakugan*) lantern—a reproduction of the one found in Katsura Rikyu. It is small and low and perfectly in keeping with the open feeling of the garden. It was mounted on a stone to raise it just above water level.

The walls of the waterfall are cast concrete to which we added a surface of rough granite. Blocks of stone are split with a chisel and the rough face is used outward. The corners were cut in an L shape and once the stones were set, the stone mason chipped off corners of adjacent stones if the height difference between them was too great. This gave the wall a unified finish.

Finally, moss was planted along with some small *Sarcandra glabra* (*senryo*) and some Japanese iris (*hanashobu*) placed in planters in two locations in the stream—a reflection of their natural habitat. Finally, *Shirakawa* sand was laid over unplanted areas.

▶ TOP TO BOTTOM: Construction of the stream and waterfall over the concrete structure.

The view across the lobby from the tea garden gives the soothing impression of a terraced mountainside.

TOP: View from the bridge over the lobby.
BOTTOM: From the middle room facing the tea garden.

CONSTRUCTING AN INDOOR TEA GARDEN

At my suggestion, Japanese-style sunken hearths (*ro*) were built into the floors of the large *tatami*-mat rooms in a different section of the second floor, so that tea ceremonies could be held there. The garden in front of these three large rooms was composed in tea garden (*cha niwa*) fashion. Though historically the tea ceremony was intended for small groups of three to five people and was the exclusive domain of the privileged classes throughout the Pre-modern era, *oyose no chakai*—large tea ceremonies of between ten and fifty people or more—constitute the bulk of tea ceremonies carried out in modern-day Japan.

This *cha niwa* is unusual in that it has a pond and stream running through it. As I mentioned earlier, this was done to create another waterfall to cascade over the nightclub below. I arranged the stream to act as a kind of *keikai*—the separation between inner and outer *roji* usually made with a bamboo fence (*yotsume gaki*)— between the three rooms that shared a view of this garden.

Unlike the larger stream, this one was made by arranging *giboku*—cast concrete made to look like cut branches of wood—directly on top of the concrete floor, to form the walls of the stream. Edges made in this fashion are called *rangui gogan* and usually use real branches of chestnut (*kuri*) or cedar (*hinoki*). The *giboku* were secured and made waterproof by stacking stone and mortar along the backside. Later the area behind the *giboku* would be filled with soil. Rounded, black pebbles called *nachiguro* are laid in loose for the bed of the stream.

In addition, we constructed an outcropping of stone extending down into the stream near to the bridge. At the stream end of this outcropping, we placed an arrangement of two small stones. Though stone settings are not a normal part of tea gardens, I felt the need for a small focal point at this location. We completed the

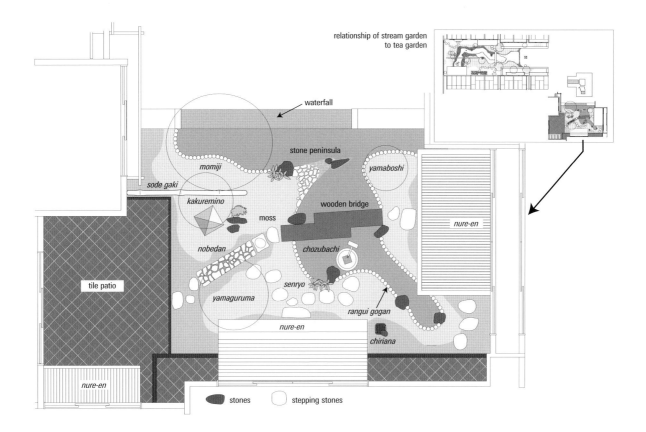

relationship of stream garden
to tea garden

waterfall

stone peninsula

momiji

yamaboshi

sode gaki

kakuremino

wooden bridge

nure-en

moss

nobedan

chozubachi

tile patio

yamaguruma

senryo

nure-en

rangui gogan

chiriana

nure-en

◗ stones   ◯ stepping stones

stonework by constructing a *nobedan* leading from the end of the bridge toward the room on the left side (when looking out toward the lobby).

We wanted to build a stone bridge for this garden, but due to scheduling problems, it was too late to haul in a large stone as the walls and windows had already been sealed. Coordination of the workflow with other trades is one problem faced in interior garden work. In place of stone we used two blocks of cedar wood about 71 x 16 x 4 inches (180 x 40 x 10 cm), burnished by a gas flame (hence the dark color). We staggered them to produce a bridge about 3.2 yards (3 m) long. The two pieces were bolted together through the side and leveled on supporting stones in the center and at both ends.

Next, the soil was brought in and layered over perlite as before; however, this time we had a more shallow space of only 20 inches (50 cm) to work with, so we mounded the soil around larger plantings as much as we could. This gave us an adequate base to plant the trees. We planted Japanese maple, *Dendropanax trifidus* (*kakuremino*), Japanese dogwood (*yamaboshi*), and wheel tree (*yamaguruma*), and laid out the stepping stones. Finally, moss was planted.

There is little to identify this as a tea garden except for a *chiriana*, the stepping stones, and the fact that the coin-shaped basin (*zeni-gata chozubachi*) is placed low as in a tea garden. Although stepping stones have been placed to allow access, the garden will mostly be admired from the three rooms and *nure-en* that surround it.

These *nure-en* platforms and the overhanging eaves (*hisashi*) were greatly extended at my insistence. The one on the right is 3.2 yards (3 m) long by 1.6 yards (1.5 m) deep, and that on the left is 4.3 yards (4 m) long by 1.3 yards (1.2 m) deep. Together, the *nure-en* and *hisashi* help integrate the interior and exterior. I believe the result is both charming and relaxing.

The veranda, tucked in behind an entrance roof, before construction.

A shallow veranda connects the distant trees to the interior space.

CONSTRUCTING A SMALL VERANDA GARDEN

A veranda garden was built by the entrance to a Japanese-style hall on the second floor of this hotel. There were no deep eaves over this veranda, so trees and plants would thrive here under direct exposure to rain and evening dew. I therefore designed the garden around a sizable Japanese maple tree with multiple trunks.

The veranda is situated behind a deep, overhanging roof that shelters a small entrance on the first floor. The back wall of the veranda is actually the top edge of that roof, a kind of parapet capped with Japanese *kawara* roofing tiles. I left that height just as it was, resulting in an open, airy feeling in this garden. It also allows the tree to be readily seen from the first floor.

The window originally had four framed panes of glass, so that there was a division down the center. I had them replaced with one large pane in the middle and a sliding glass door on either side. This created an uninterrupted view in the center.

As with the indoor gardens, the idea behind this veranda was a "large-scale bonsai." Although this veranda is outdoors and therefore under normal light and water conditions, the situation at ground level presents the same problem—water must drain from the roots and the growth of those roots is restricted by an enclosure. The soil must therefore retain moisture as long as possible. Accordingly, the same mix of regular and bonsai-specific soils was used over a perlite base.

An otherwise dead space becomes a beautiful garden.

Since this space was shallow at only 12 inches (30 cm) deep, I mounded soil to a height of 20 inches (50 cm) at the point where the root ball of the maple was to be planted. I embedded an *ikekomi*-style six-sided lantern close to this, packing the soil around the base. To hold this soil in place, I embedded roofing tiles in a scalloped pattern—a typical technique in Japanese gardens—that serves both as a retaining wall and as a clean method of keeping different materials from getting mixed into each other. Outside of this I formed one small island of soil in order to plant a white enkianthus (*dodan tsutsuji*). The edge in this case is left plain. Moss is planted over all the mounded soil area, and the remaining areas are filled with *Shirakawa* sand and raked.

To cover an unsightly skylight on the right, I planted Thunberg's meadowsweet (*yuki yanagi*); but by the third year it had died and so I replaced it with a bamboo fence. The only other "problem" has been that the maple has thrived and there have been some complaints that it casts too much shadow on the interior.

Finally, I borrowed a strip of floor adjacent to the inside of the window and framed it with polished marble. Then I used the same sand as outside to fill this inside space, visually drawing the garden past the window frame and into the interior.

A *kare sansui* garden, deep in the mountains.

TERRACE GARDEN OF FUJIISO HOTEL

Fujiiso is a traditional-style inn built of reinforced concrete, its tiered four-story structure clinging to the sloping face of a valley deep in the mountains. The terrace, some
11 yards (10 m) wide, had been unimpressively planted with shrubbery along the
edge. Compared to the magnificence of the surrounding scenery, it looked totally
misplaced. To complement and contrast the beauty of the mountains behind it, I
designed the garden there as a flat dry landscape, featuring in the foreground a
winding walkway of round stones with red mortar joints.

The terrace before construction.

CREATING THE GARDEN

After removing the old hedges and extended parapet, openings in the concrete
were closed with wooden planks.

The stone walkway began by choosing rather thin stones—1¼ to 4 inches (3 to
10 cm)—that have one relatively flat side. We used *koban-ishi* and *tama-ishi*. The
overall shape was drawn in white paint, and we began at one end by washing the
concrete and coating it with a material that promotes adhesion between the concrete and mortar. Immediately we started to lay in a bed of mortar, about 6 inches
(15 cm) thick, and set the stones. Remember to clean the stones in advance and to
wash any mortar off the top surface of the stones before it sets.

Once the entire walkway was set, we placed several medium-size stones in the area to be surrounded by sand. These stones had one side cut flat so that they could sit on the concrete and look buried, in a natural way, with just the depth of the sand.

We also placed an *ikekomi toro*. Although this type is normally buried, here again we cut the bottom very flat and stuck it to the concrete with epoxy glue made for stone-to-stone adhesion.

Next, we constructed our *Ryoanji gaki* (see details following), in 2.1-yard (2-m) sections, and placed it on stands constructed from steel pipe and sheet steel. The stand sits directly on the concrete and the legs of the fence slide over it.

Next, we covered the surface with a bed of sand that is between 1¼ and 4 inches (3 and 10 cm) deep. The reason for the great difference is the grading of the underlying cement. It is always necessary to level the sand even in those rare times when the ground underneath cannot be leveled.

Finally, we returned to the stone walkway with a mixture of mortar and red pigment and carefully filled in the joints around the stones to give them a bright effect. The color will eventually fade and will need to be replenished.

■ CONSTRUCTING THE *RYOANJI GAKI*

This fence takes its name from the original located on the grounds of Ryoanji temple in Kyoto.

1. Decide the size of the fence (in this case about 35.4 inches/90 cm tall by 2.1-yard/2-m long portable sections). Take two vertical wooden poles of about 4 inches (10 cm) diameter and notch the top ends and one more point about 6 inches (15 cm) from the bottom ends.

2. Split a 3- to 4-inch (8- to 10-cm) piece of bamboo four ways and clean off the interior nodes. Insert one piece of quarter-cut bamboo in the top notch and one in the bottom. Secure to the post with nails and wire.

3. Begin the cross members by putting two of the quarters together with the green side outward and tying them with wire.

4. Tie this to the horizontal members of the fence with wire at an angle. The bottom of the angled piece should extend past the bottom horizontal post by about 4 inches (10 cm).

5. Decide the pitch—usually 8 to 12 inches (20 to 30 cm)—between these and the next quarters and repeat the process of tying them to the horizontals.

6. When one direction is complete, continue the process in the opposite direction, creating a uniform crisscross pattern as you go. The shape of the crisscross should form horizontal—not vertical—diamonds. Start the opposite piece so that it overlaps the edge of the piece already connected. As with other fences described in this book, pull a level string across the frame to check the height of the crossed points.

1·2

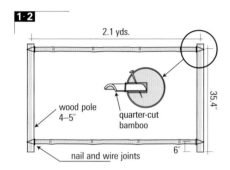

2.1 yds.

35.4"

wood pole
4–5"

quarter-cut
bamboo

nail and wire joints

6"

2

split into 4 pieces with *nata* or splitter

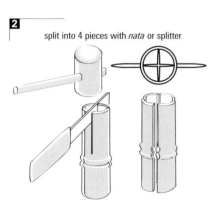

3

4·5·6

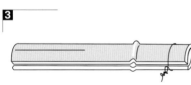

12"

tie joints with copper wire

check level of crossed points

7. When finished with the diagonal pieces, take a half-cut bamboo of about 4 inches (10 cm) diameter and tie it over the front and back of the upper horizontal member. Then place a third half above this to cap it off, creating a kind of clover shape when viewed from the end. Tie it together with wire or *shuronawa*. This final top cap should be clean and straight. Tying it together tightly will straighten out any bends in the fence.

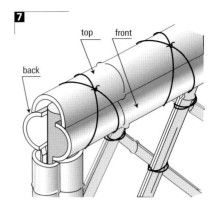

8. On top of the bottom horizontal member place a half-cut bamboo on the front and one half on the backside and tie it with wire or *shuronawa*. Place three halves over the vertical members on each end in the same manner as the top.

9. Then take the copper wire or *shuronawa* and tie off every crisscross joint along the entire fence. Wire is easier to use for beginners than *shuronawa*, but I often prefer wire because it presents a quieter appearance overall.

10. In the case of this fence, the concrete surface underneath prohibited burying the post. In order to stand the fence up, we had steel stands fabricated from 20 x 20-inch (50 x 50-cm) sheet steel with a ¾-inch (2-cm) diameter by 27.5-inch (70-cm) long steel pipe welded vertically to the center. We added two additional bamboo posts to the back of each section of fence and punched out the nodes. Then we slid the fence over the steel stands and covered the base with sand.

Another reason the fence is made in sections is to make it easy to remove and store every winter, when 3 to 4 yards (3 to 4 m) of snow blankets these mountains. At that time we also cover the entire veranda with grass mats or vinyl sheeting to keep the sand and stone from being damaged by snow-removal equipment.

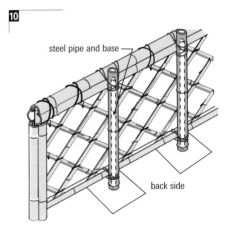

GENERAL TECHNIQUES

ASSEMBLING AND PLACING STONE LANTERNS

Three basic types of lantern commonly seen in the Japanese garden are the pedestal type (*tachi-gata*), ground-inserted type (*ikekomi*), and the so-called snow-viewing type (*yukimi-geta*). Here I will explain briefly each type, its use, and how to assemble it.

■ Setting a *Kasuga* Stone Lantern

The *Kasuga* lantern is the most popular pedestal type (though the oldest style is the *Taimaji*), and so closely associated with this type that many refer to pedestal lanterns as *Kasuga* lanterns. The original lantern is from Mt. Kasuga in Nara. Pedestal types are composed of six parts: pedestal (*kiso*), column (*sao*), middle platform (*chudai*), fire or light box (*hibukuro*), shade (*kasa*) and orb (*hoju*). The *Kasuga* lantern has a six-sided pedestal, middle platform, light box, and shade. The column is round. Lanterns were originally brought into the garden from the Buddhist temples, where they are still a prominent feature. Only pedestal-type lanterns are found in sizes from 1 to 11 yards

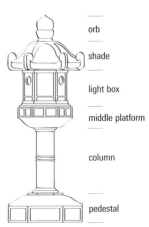

Lantern parts and assembly with a crane.

(1 to 10 m) tall and four, six, or eight sides. The lantern in the photo on this page is about 3.2 yards (3 m) tall.

1. The orientation of the lantern is decided first. The "face" of the lantern is usually the largest open side of the light box and one side of the six-sided pieces. Modern lanterns are often made with an arrow on the inside surfaces, showing which side is the front of the lantern.

2. The ground under the lantern is pounded flat. A base of mortar or cement may be used, but in an earthquake-prone country like Japan, I usually use rough stones over the packed soil. When the earth shakes, the movement of the stones absorbs the shock and the lantern is less likely to tip over.

3. After the pedestal, the shaft and middle platform are centered and placed above it. At this point, the level is checked and adjusted. Adjustment is made by pushing in soil or small stones under the pedestal.

4. Next come the light box, shade, and orb. Finding the center is difficult and takes patience. Lanterns made in the Medieval era were fitted with fat pegs and holes to make assembly easier and to resist lateral shock. The peg and hole becomes gradually more slender until it disappears entirely in the Pre-modern era. This is one method of identifying the age of a lantern. Other methods of identification involve points like taller orbs (Pre-modern) and light box sizes (the larger the box in relation to the column, the older the lantern).

5. A wooden frame with paper—like a small *shoji*—is fitted to the larger rectangular openings and held in place with a sliver of bamboo. This practice stems from the fact that candles or oil lamps used in the lantern were easily blown out. The practice is continued today even if the lantern is not used or has been fitted with an electric light.

■ Setting an *Ikekomi*-style Lantern

This type of lantern has no pedestal (although it often has a small flare at the base) and is buried directly in the ground. As with the *Kasuga* lantern, the *Oribe* lantern is so closely associated with this style that it is often used as the generic name. This is one of the only lanterns named after a person instead of the place of its original use. That person, Furuta Oribe, was a tea master from the sixteenth century who is almost as famous as Sen no Rikyu for his innovations and style in the tea ceremony. It is thought that Oribe (and many others in the era) was a Christian, or heavily influenced by the religion. The *Oribe* lantern is also known as a *hina-gata* or Christian lantern due to its cross-like shape and markings like *lhq*, pronounced *qahal*, ("assembly" in Hebrew) often found on the pedestal.

Oribe's motivation for designing or using this lantern probably came from the desire to have something smaller and simpler than the pedestal type. It has the advantage of easy height adjustment by burying more or less of the column. This lantern is generally found in a square or cylindrical shape and never found in large sizes. It is usually a yard (1 m) or less in height.

1. To set the *ikekomi* lantern, decide the orientation and dig a hole at least 12 inches (30 cm) deep and wider than the column. The broad side of the pedestal and the largest opening in the light box face forward.

2. Place the column in the hole and force some stones between the column and the inside of the hole. Place the middle platform on the column temporarily and check the level.

3. Remove the middle platform and push the stones in tight. Start filling the hole slowly and pound the dirt down deeply and completely with a wooden pole or some other narrow instrument. Make sure there are no gaps.

4. Set the middle platform, the light box, shade, and orb just as you would for the pedestal type.

■ Setting a Snow-Viewing Lantern (*Yukimi-gata*)

Despite the name, this lantern is associated with ponds or the surface of water. If there is no water, this lantern looks out of place. Although it is sometimes used outside this context, I advise against it. In fact, as pond gardens have become increasingly rarer in Japan, the *yukimi* lantern and its cousin the *mizubotaru* (or *koto-ji*) lantern are becoming more difficult to use in their proper context.

There are two basic types of this lantern: four-legged and three-legged. The main characteristic of this lantern is its large, round shade. The height of this lantern is usually less than a yard (1 m), but large lanterns are sometimes seen.

To stand this lamp, decide the orientation, then level the ground and tamp down the soil.

For the four-legged type, simply stand the base-legs and then stack the light box, shade, and orb (if there is one). The middle platform is usually attached to the legs. The legs should stand so that two legs face front. If the shade is round, its orientation does not matter. If the lantern is six sided, one side should face front.

The three-legged type is very tricky. The legs are independent and connected by a block that they slot into. It is rather difficult to get the balance of the legs just right. Too close together and the lantern will be unstable and difficult to level. Too wide apart and the legs will spread further when the heavy upper parts are assembled. The correct orientation is one leg placed directly in front. The legs should also be buried about 4 inches (10 cm) to keep the lantern from tipping over.

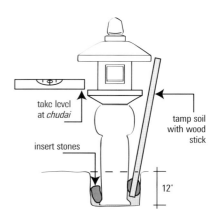

Base showing peg (left) and completed lantern (right).

Assembly of a three-legged *yukimi-gata*.

The finished lantern.

CHAPTER

5

Special Touches, Restoration, and Maintenance

My home prefecture of Nagano is cold and dry in winter, and protective *fuyugakoi* (winter enclosures) made of straw have long been a fixture of the winter landscape. Covering the base of the tree raises the temperature only a few degrees, but it helps to retain moisture and keep the tree from drying out in the winter months. It also serves to collect insects that descend from the branches to the ground as the weather gets cold. A similar device of wrapping the trunk of the tree to collect insects (*mushi taji*) is found throughout Japan. In that case a mat of straw is simply wrapped around the trunk of the tree about a yard (1 m) from the ground. Come springtime, the straw is removed and burned. The practice of wrapping the base of the tree is only done in relatively cold areas that receive less than a yard (1 m) of snow in winter. It is not done where the snow gets deep.

For some the main aspect is the decorative one, and *fuyugakoi* are often employed by hotels and restaurants to dress up the garden in winter. I make my *fuyugakoi* with the rushes (*igusa*) ordinarily used to weave *tatami*-mat facings because it makes for a more refined look than straw. But any kind of straw of a meter or more in length will do. On the following pages I show a basic wrapping made of rice straw.

■ MAKING A BASIC *FUYUGAKOI*

1. Clean as much debris from the straw as possible by brushing through it with your hand. Then make six bundles of about 1⅔ inch (4 cm) diameter each (a larger tree will require more bundles) and tie each just tight enough so they don't fall apart.

2. Take some thick rope and wrap it several times around the trunk of the tree, about 8 inches (20 cm) from the base. When the straw is fastened against the tree, it presses against the rope and bends outward.

3. Now take each bundle of straw and wet it thoroughly in a bucket of water. If the straw is not softened by wetting, it will snap rather than bend.

4. Take the bundles and stack them against the tree at an angle, with the thicker end of the straw on the ground. Push on the straw to bend it toward the rope wrapped around the trunk.

5. Take a piece of *shuronawa* cord that has been soaked in water, and double-wrap it around all the bundles, spreading the straw against the trunk as you go. When you have a thick, even mat of straw, knot the cord and cut it. Then repeat with another row of cord about ¾ inch (2 cm) higher than the first one.

Looking somewhat like the dancing brooms in *Fantasia*, the various *fuyugakoi* pictured here add a delightful, formal touch to the winter garden scenery.

Ropes and straw for a *fuyugakoi*

1

2

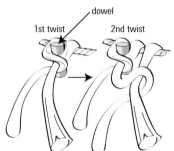

3

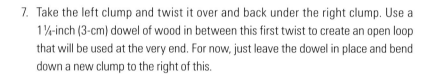

4

5

dowel

1st twist   2nd twist

6. Now begin braiding the straw by bending over two clumps of straw, about half the thickness of the mat, at the point where the *shuronawa* holds it against the tree. Grab one clump in each hand firmly.

7. Take the left clump and twist it over and back under the right clump. Use a 1¼-inch (3-cm) dowel of wood in between this first twist to create an open loop that will be used at the very end. For now, just leave the dowel in place and bend down a new clump to the right of this.

8. While holding the previous right clump now in your left hand, grasp this new bent-over clump in your right hand. Now twist the clump in your left hand over and back under the new clump in your right hand (a repeat of the first twist but without the dowel).

9. Grasp this new twist in your left hand and bend a new clump with your right hand. Repeat the twist with left clump over and back under the right. Continue this twisting until a full row of straw is braided around the tree.

10. Now you have returned to the point with the dowel. Pull out the dowel and push the last clump (this should be in your left hand) through the top of the loop that remains after removing the dowel.

11. Pull it through with your right hand, and with your left hand grasp the end of the looped straw and pull them both to make a tight knot. This is the end of the first braid.

12. Now tie a double loop of polyester or nylon chord around the straw—which is still standing upright against the tree—about 4 inches (10 cm) higher than the braided straw. The polyester won't grab the straw and pull it around as *shuronawa* would. The straw should entirely cover the trunk of the tree and should not be twisted.

6

7

10

13

15

16

13. Next, take two adjacent clumps of straw that stick out from the bottom of the braid, cross them over each other, and tie them together with a long length of *shuronawa* cord. Tie them with one end of the cord and knot it.

14. Now take the two adjacent clumps and cross them. Take the cord and loop it over and under the crossed section to hold them together while you grasp the next two clumps. The cord is now connected to four clumps of crossed straw.

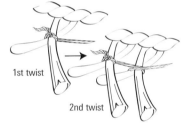
1st twist

2nd twist

15. Keep repeating this around the tree until you have a chain of cord with crossed straw in between. When you return to the starting point, knot the cord to the first section so that the chain is completely closed.

16. Take your sheers and cut the crossed straw ¾ to 1¼ inches (2 to 3 cm) from the knotted cord. Keep cutting around the tree, and when finished, fan out each section so that the tips just about touch each other.

17. Tie another double loop of polyester cord right above the braided straw. Knot the cord and cut it.

18. Take your sheers and cut the straw around the trunk of the tree in a straight line ¾ to 1¼ inches (2 to 3 cm) above the top polyester cord.

19. Now remove the ties still holding the six large clumps of straw and fan out the straw in an even skirt around the tree.

20. Finally, cut the skirt in an even circle and clean off any remaining debris. Stick all the debris under the skirt to help trap moisture there.

18

19

20

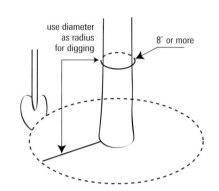

use diameter
as radius
for digging

8" or more

■ TRANSPLANTING TREES

One important aspect of maintenance is replacing and transplanting trees. Generally speaking, deciduous trees are best transplanted after their leaves have fallen or before they come out, and evergreens around the time of budding. Here I demonstrate with a zelkova (*keyaki*).

1. The width of the root ball to be cut out will depend on the diameter of the tree trunk. As a rule of thumb, the diameter of the tree is measured with a cord and this cord is used as the radius of a circle that is drawn around the tree. This rule works for any tree with a diameter of 8 inches (20 cm) or more. For trees with a narrow trunk, use 1.5 to 3 times the diameter as the radius.

2. The proper way to transplant a large tree is to begin at least one to three years in advance by preparing the roots (the larger the tree, the longer the preparation time). This is done by digging out the soil around the roots to the decided circumference. Notch the thick roots with a saw or, better yet, strip off a section of the bark and the membrane underneath. Cut some of the smaller roots. The roots close to the tree are woody and will not absorb moisture from the soil after the tree is dug out. To compensate for this, stripping the root promotes the growth of fine new roots close to the trunk that will absorb water. Rebury the stripped roots and cut off between 20 to 50 percent of the leaves to help the tree retain moisture.

3. When the time comes to dig out the root ball, dig a trench alongside large enough for a person to get into. As you cut into the ground and encounter the roots, be sure to cut any thick root cleanly with a saw. Making a mess of the cut will endanger the tree. It is also advisable to sharpen your spade to give it a better cutting edge as you dig.

4. Keep digging and cutting until you notice the roots becoming scarcer, then turn in toward the center of the tree and start to dig underneath it. Remember that deciduous trees will have shallower roots and evergreens have a deep and thick tap root.

5. Now that most of the root ball is cut out, wrap the soil with hemp rope to keep it from falling away from the roots. If the soil is sandy, use a mesh, and if the root ball will be exposed overnight, use straw or hemp mat and wrap the rope over that. This will be soaked with water to keep the roots from drying out. Be sure the material you use allows air to pass through. Hemp can be reburied with the roots and will deteriorate naturally over time.

6. Wrap the rootball first around the circumference and then over and under like a ball of twine.

7. Attach a rope to the trunk and pull the tree over, or use a crane and sling to lift out the tree and set it on its side. If the leaf canopy is very large, tie the branches together to prevent them from snapping, especially if you need to transport the tree by truck.

8. At the new location dig a hole up to twice the size of the root ball. The best chance for survival requires that the soil at the new site match the original soil. If this is not available, hold the tree above the new hole with a crane and knock off as much of the soil as you can. Mix this together with the soil in the new area plus at least 10 percent leafy organic matter to help retain moisture.

9. Soil is first piled in a cone at the bottom of the new hole. This is done because the soil around the center of the root ball, the most difficult place to reach when digging and wrapping, often falls out. This leaves a concave space under the root ball that must be filled with soil. Leaving a large unfilled gap under the base of the tree will kill it.

10. Orient the tree while the sling is still attached. Rotate to face the "best side" toward the principal viewpoint.

11. When about half the soil is replaced around the tree, fill it with water until the soil is muddy. Put one foot on the root ball and grasp the tree trunk. Wiggle the tree around to set it and further eliminate the chance of gaps. Then fill in all the soil.

12. A ring of soil is often made around newly transplanted trees as a basin for retaining water. Water the tree heavily every day or two for the first six months—less if the tree is transplanted in winter. Mix the water with a fertilizer in a proportion of one to one hundred and use it every third day or so.

13. Finally, if there are strong winds in the area, tie the tree down to bamboo or wooden poles to keep it from shifting around. The roots will grow better if the tree is not being pushed back and forth. For deciduous trees, one year may be enough; up to three years for pines. It is also a good idea to cover the tree with a net for the first six months or so.

14. For about one week after the transplant, the old growth should be falling away. New leaf should start to appear after that. If the old leaf fails to fall away and seems to be limply hanging from the branches, it is a sign that the roots are drying out (be careful: over-watering or lack of oxygen will also kill the roots and keep them from absorbing moisture, to the same effect). In this case it is best to strip off all the old leaves by hand. This keeps moisture from evaporating from the tree and gives the roots a chance to take hold.

Care should be exercised about which branches are supported and an adequate number of ropes used.

A repository for gods (*kami*), kadomatsu stand at the entrance to this hotel.

YUKITSURI

Yukitsuri is a type of winter enclosure whereby branches are suspended on ropes radiating down from a tall central post that has been placed close to the trunk of the tree. The purpose is to add support to pine branches that would otherwise snap under the weight of winter snow.

KADOMATSU

Gardeners in Japan also provide New Year's decorations as a sideline to garden making. The traditional New Year *kadomatsu* ornament is placed at the front entrance of most homes and businesses during the *makunouchi* season—from December 28 to January 7.

Kadomatsu is made by cutting three bamboo poles with a diameter of about 4 inches (10 cm) each, into two or three different heights. The top of the bamboo is cut at a steep angle. The bamboo is tied together with the tallest in the back and all the cut angles facing forward. This group can be placed in any type of base if it is covered. Traditionally we use cut branches tied around the bamboo with string. The area surrounding the bamboo is filled with pine branches and a sprig of plum. More elaborate arrangements, such as the ones illustrated here, may include such items as a straw skirt, *mizuhiki* string decorations, *shimekazari* rope, and *gohei* zigzag paper decorations.

RESTORING A BAMBOO FENCE

As I mentioned in Chapter 3, mold and mildew are the greatest enemies of bamboo. This is what turns it black and eventually rots it. Coating the fence thoroughly with a fungicide, bleach, or lightweight oil when it is first built goes a long way to suppressing the growth of mold. Even then, it pays to clean the fence and recoat it every three to five years. If your fence has turned black, follow these steps to restore it:

1. Hose the fence down thoroughly. Use a fungicide or bleach mixed half and half with water and brush it heavily over the fence. Bleach is cheap and works quite well.

2. After the bleach has had some time to work, wash it off with a hose.

3. The fence should be restored to a gray-white tone. Let it dry well, then coat it again. This time use 100% bleach or fungicide—or if you want a deeper color, coat it with oil. The oil will deepen the color while adding protection.

LEFT TO RIGHT: Cleaning the fence, killing the mold, and coating it to keep it looking fresh.

MAINTENANCE AND RESTORATION

The Japanese aesthetic prizes cleanliness above all else. Maintaining a Japanese garden primarily consists of cleaning, watering, trimming, and weeding. It is said in Zen Buddhism that training begins and ends with cleaning. There is nothing so beautiful as a temple, the wood of which has a patina from daily cleaning, and this is just as true for any residence no matter how modest. The Japanese have traditionally kept their gardens free of weeds by sweeping with bamboo brooms, uprooting young weeds in the process, and plucking debris with chopsticks (*chiribashi*). Below, I have included a small table to give your maintenance duties a seasonal focus.

Winter	If humidity falls below 50%, water every day between 10 A.M. and 3 P.M. to avoid freezing.
	If moss is planted, prevent freezing by laying straw or leaves over the moss.
	Spray general insecticide about three times during the winter.
	Plan any changes to make in the spring.
	Take precautions to protect water features and water systems from freezing damage.
	Clean and rake sand. Blowers are also good for cleaning sand. Lightweight, inexpensive ones are readily available.
Spring	Water demand is at its highest, so water morning and night.
	Planting and replanting.
	Take off the straw wrapped around tree trunks in fall and burn it.
	Fertilize.
	Trim trees, pluck pine buds.
	Drain and clean the pond, filters, and other water features.
	Repair the pond and other water features where needed. Reset stones.
	Replace any dead moss and pull weeds.
	Cut the azalea hedges about ¾ inch (2 cm) after the flowers have come out but before they die off.
	Clean and rake sand.

Summer	Water morning and night.
	Weeding.
	Targeted insecticide.
	Mow grass. If moss is long enough for strands to fall over, trim it.
	In areas where sun is too strong, shade the moss with bamboo mats or other screening to prevent burning.
	Clean and rake sand.
Fall	Keep watering deciduous trees heavily until leaves begin to fall. Heavy watering produces good color. Otherwise, watering is moderate.
	Rake fallen leaves. Keep in a vinyl bag for use during the winter and to create mulch.
	Pruning after the leaves fall. Branches are easy to see and easy to cut on deciduous trees. Evergreens and conifers should also be trimmed and pinched.
	Trim hedges about ¾ inch (2 cm).
	Wrap trees in straw to trap insects. Set *yukitsuri* in snowy climates. Set *fuyugakoi*.
	Clean and rake sand. Every three to five years, gather up the rougher sand. Remove the finer and dirtier sand and replace with new material.

NOTE: The frequency of various types of maintenance will vary based on local conditions, micro-conditions in the garden, and the condition of each tree or group of plantings. For example, the dry, cold climate of the area where I live demands more attention to watering, whereas a rainy climate requires more attention to issues of rot and soil erosion. Micro-condition requirements involve treating specific areas *within* the garden differently. A sloped area should be handled differently than a flat area, a sheltered area differently than an area receiving high-winds, an area receiving long exposure to sunshine differently than one heavily shaded, and so on. Maintenance based on plant conditions include considering such factors as the age of a tree (younger or recent transplants require more watering), or the amount of pruning (hedges more often than trees) or mowing (Kentucky Bluegrass more, Zoysia less).

ACKNOWLEDGMENTS

I would like to express my gratitude to the following people for their tireless work on this project: Tetsuo Kuramochi, who first proposed the idea for this book; Joseph Cali, who fleshed out the concept, worked closely with the text, and drew the illustrations; Kay Yokota, who translated large passages of the work; Matt Cotterill, who handled the editing of the text; and Kazuhiko Miki and Masumi Akiyama, who conceived the design.

Motomi Oguchi

■ ■ ■

I would like to thank Oguchi-sensei for his patience over the several years it took to realize this book, as I dotted the *i*'s and crossed the *t*'s. Thanks also to Professor Yoshiki Toda for his help in understanding the Izumo style and other aspects of Oguchi-sensei's work; to Yukinori Aida for his kind help with supplementary translations, and to Gen Koichi for his assistance with the *fuyugakoi* instructions. Finally, I would like to acknowledge all the gardeners and professors who never hesitate to share their knowledge and work with an inquisitive student.

Joseph Cali

CREDITS

- All photographs by Motomi Oguchi, except those of the *sanmatta* photo (page 102) and the *fuyugakoi* (pages 122–23), which are by Joseph Cali.
- All illustrations by Joseph Cali.

(英文版) 日本庭園の作り方
Create Your Own Japanese Garden

2007 年 4 月 25 日　第 1 刷発行

著　者　小口基實、ジョセフ・キャリ
翻　訳　横田 恵
発行者　富田 充
発行所　講談社インターナショナル株式会社
　　　　〒112-8652　東京都文京区音羽 1-17-14
　　　　電話　03-3944-6493 (編集部)
　　　　　　　03-3944-6492 (マーケティング部・業務部)
　　　　ホームページ　www.kodansha-intl.com

印刷・製本所　大日本印刷株式会社